my revision notes

AS Edexcel History

# IDEOLOGY, CONFLICT AND RETREAT

## THE USA IN ASIA, 1950–73

Robin Bunce
Laura Gallagher

HODDER EDUCATION
AN HACHETTE UK COMPANY

Every effort has been made to trace all copyright holders, but if any have been inadvertently overlooked the Publishers will be pleased to make the necessary arrangements at the first opportunity.

Although every effort has been made to ensure that website addresses are correct at time of going to press, Hodder Education cannot be held responsible for the content of any website mentioned in this book. It is sometimes possible to find a relocated web page by typing in the address of the home page for a website in the URL window of your browser.

Hachette UK's policy is to use papers that are natural, renewable and recyclable products and made from wood grown in sustainable forests. The logging and manufacturing processes are expected to conform to the environmental regulations of the country of origin.

**Orders:** please contact Bookpoint Ltd, 130 Milton Park, Abingdon, Oxon OX14 4SB. Telephone: +44 (0)1235 827720. Fax: +44 (0)1235 400454. Lines are open 9.00a.m.–5.00p.m., Monday to Saturday, with a 24-hour message answering service. Visit our website at www.hoddereducation.co.uk.

© Robin Bunce and Laura Gallagher 2012

First published in 2012 by
Hodder Education,
An Hachette UK company
London NW1 3BH

Impression number      5  4  3

Year                   2016  2015  2014

All rights reserved. Apart from any use permitted under UK copyright law, no part of this publication may be reproduced or transmitted in any form or by any means, electronic or mechanical, including photocopying and recording, or held within any information storage and retrieval system, without permission in writing from the publisher or under licence from the Copyright Licensing Agency Limited. Further details of such licences (for reprographic reproduction) may be obtained from the Copyright Licensing Agency Limited, Saffron House, 6–10 Kirby Street, London EC1N 8TS.

**Cover image** © Aleksandar Mijatovic – Fotolia
Typeset in 11/13 Stempel Schneidler Std by Datapage (India) Pvt. Ltd.
Artwork by Datapage and Gray Publishing
Printed and bound in Spain
A catalogue record for this title is available from the British Library
ISBN 978 1 444 17751 0

# Contents

|   |   |
|---|---|
| Introduction | 2 |

**Revised** **Section 1:** The Korean War, 1950–53: causes, course and consequences — 4

- The causes of the Korean War: the Cold War — 4
- The causes of the Korean War: North Korean aggression — 6
- The course of the Korean War, June–November 1950 — 8
- The course of the Korean War, November 1950–April 1951 — 10
- Armistice negotiations — 12
- The impact of the Korean War — 14
- Exam focus — 16

**Revised** **Section 2:** The ideological struggle in south-east Asia in the early 1950s — 18

- Imperial decline in south-east Asia — 18
- US involvement in south-east Asia, 1950–54 — 20
- The Geneva Peace Conference, 1954 — 22
- The foundation of SEATO — 24
- Exam focus — 26

**Revised** **Section 3:** Growing US participation in Vietnam, 1954–68 — 28

- Eisenhower: limited intervention — 28
- The relationship between the USA and Diem — 30
- Kennedy: motivation for continuing involvement in Vietnam — 32
- Kennedy: deepening involvement in Vietnam — 34
- Johnson: initial escalation — 36
- The nature of the Vietnam War — 38
- Johnson: massive escalation — 40
- The significance of the Tet Offensive — 42
- Public opinion and the cost of the War — 44
- Exam focus — 46

**Revised** **Section 4:** The Nixon presidency and the withdrawal of US forces, 1969–73 — 48

- Nixon and Vietnamisation — 48
- Achieving 'peace with honour': Nixon's military strategy — 50
- Achieving 'peace with honour': Nixon's diplomatic strategy — 52
- The impact of the anti-war movement — 54
- The end of the Vietnam War — 56
- Exam focus — 58

| | |
|---|---|
| Glossary | 60 |
| Timeline | 63 |
| Answers | 65 |

# Introduction

## About Unit 1

Unit 1 is worth 50 per cent of your AS level. It requires detailed knowledge of a historical period and the ability to explain the causes, consequences and significance of historical events. There are no sources in the Unit 1 exam and therefore all marks available are awarded for use of your own knowledge.

In the exam, you are required to answer two questions from a range of options. The exam lasts for 1 hour and 20 minutes, unless you have been awarded extra time. The questions are all worth 30 marks and therefore you should divide your time equally between the questions.

The questions you answer must be on different topics. This book deals exclusively with topic D6: Ideology, Conflict and Retreat: The USA in Asia, 1950–73. However, you must also be prepared to answer a question on another topic.

The exam will test your ability to:

- select information that focuses on the question
- organise this information to provide an answer to the question
- show range and depth in the examples you provide
- analyse the significance of the information used to reach an overall judgement.

## Ideology, Conflict and Retreat: The USA in Asia, 1950–73

The exam board specifies that students should study four general areas as part of this topic.

1. The Korean War, 1950–53: causes, course and consequences.
2. The ideological struggle in south-east Asia in the early 1950s.
3. Growing US participation in Vietnam, 1954–68.
4. The Nixon presidency and the withdrawal of US forces, 1969–73.

## How to use this book

This book has been designed to help you to develop the knowledge and skills necessary to succeed in the exam. The book is divided into four sections – one for each general area of the course. Each section is made up of a series of topics organised into double-page spreads. On the left-hand page, you will find a summary of the key content you need to learn. Words in bold in the key content are defined in the glossary (see pages 60–62). On the right-hand page, you will find exam-focused activities. Together, these two strands of the book will take you through the knowledge and skills essential for exam success.

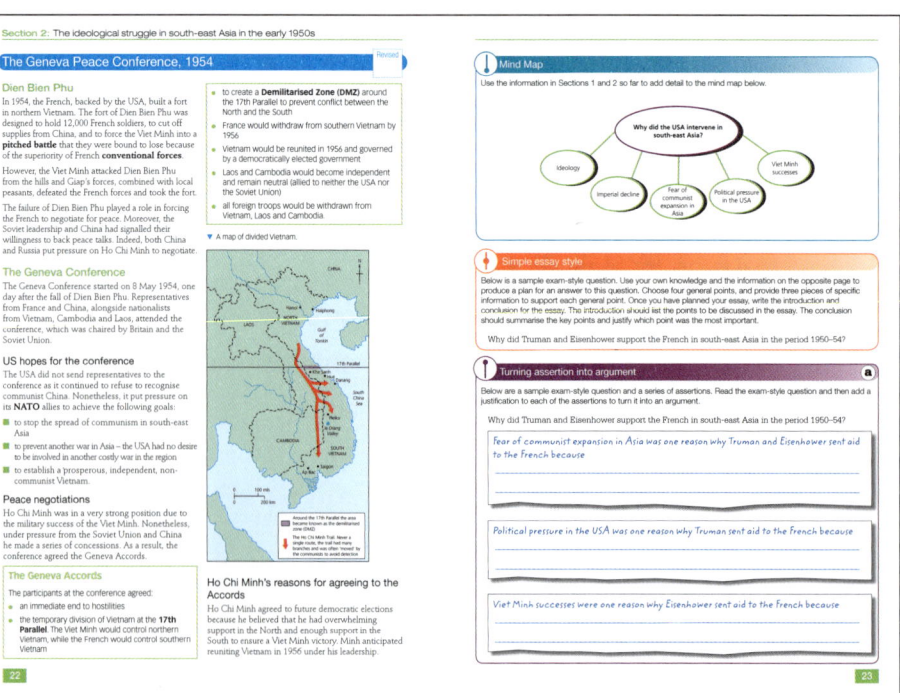

There are three levels of exam-focused activities:

- Band 1 activities are designed to develop the foundational skills needed to pass the exam. These have a turquoise heading and this symbol:
- Band 2 activities are designed to build on the skills developed in Band 1 activities and to help you achieve a C grade. These have an orange heading and this symbol:
- Band 3 activities are designed to enable you to access the highest grades. These have a purple heading and this symbol:

Some of the activities have answers or suggested answers on pages 65–68 and have the following symbol to indicate this: (a)

Others are intended for you to complete in pairs and assess by comparing answers. These do not have answers provided.

Each section ends with an exam-style question and model A-grade answer with examiner's commentary. This should give you guidance on what is required to achieve the top grades.

You can keep track of your revision by ticking off each topic heading in the book, or by ticking the checklist on the contents page. Tick each box when you have:

- revised and understood a topic
- completed the activities.

## Mark scheme

For some of the activities in the book it will be useful to refer to the mark scheme for the unit. Below is the mark scheme for Unit 1.

| Level | Marks | Description |
|---|---|---|
| 1 | 1–6 | • Lacks focus on the question.<br>• Limited factual accuracy.<br>• Highly generalised.<br>*Level 1 answers are highly simplistic, irrelevant or vague.* |
| 2 | 7–12 | • General points with some focus on the question.<br>• Some accurate and relevant supporting evidence.<br>*Level 2 answers might tell the story without addressing the question, or address the question without providing supporting examples.* |
| 3 | 13–18 | • General points that focus on the question.<br>• Accurate support, but this may be either only partly relevant or lacking detail, or both.<br>• Attempted analysis.<br>*Level 3 answers attempt to focus on the question, but have significant areas of weakness. For example, the focus on the question may drift, the answer may lack specific examples, or parts of the essay may simply tell the story. Answers which do not deal with factors that are stated in the question cannot achieve higher than Level 3.* |
| 4 | 19–24 | • General points that clearly focus on the question and show understanding of the most important factors involved.<br>• Accurate, relevant and detailed supporting evidence.<br>• Analysis.<br>*Level 4 answers clearly attempt to answer the question and demonstrate a detailed and wide-ranging knowledge of the period studied.* |
| 5 | 25–30 | • As Level 4.<br>• Sustained analysis.<br>*Level 5 answers are thorough and detailed. They clearly engage with the question and offer a balanced and carefully reasoned argument, which is sustained throughout the essay.* |

# Section 1:
# The Korean War, 1950–53: causes, course and consequences

## The causes of the Korean War: the Cold War

### The origins of the Cold War

After defeating the **Axis Powers** in the Second World War, mutual suspicion, ideological differences and competition for influence in the post-war world led to a breakdown in the **Grand Alliance** and the emergence of the Cold War.

> **The Cold War**
>
> The Cold War describes a period of economic and ideological competition between the USA and the **Soviet Union** which started after the Second World War in 1945 and ended around the time of the collapse of the Soviet Union in 1991. Although US and Soviet troops never fought each other, there was military competition between the two powers in the form of an **arms race** and **proxy wars**.

### Superpower competition

By the late 1940s it was becoming increasingly clear that the world was dominated by the USA and the Soviet Union. These two **superpowers** represented competing economic and political systems:

|  | Political system | Economic system |
| --- | --- | --- |
| USA | Democracy:<br>• Free and regular elections allow the people to choose a government from competing political parties.<br>• Individual rights are protected by law. | Capitalism:<br>• The government plays a small role in the economy.<br>• Goods and services are provided by privately owned businesses. |
| Soviet Union | Single-party government:<br>• The Communist Party is the only legal party and dominates the government.<br>• Political freedom is restricted; citizens have very limited rights to express themselves or to protest. | State socialism:<br>• The government controls the country's economy.<br>• Goods and services are produced according to a government plan and sold at fixed prices. |

Both superpowers gained a **sphere of influence** following the War. The Soviet Union dominated Eastern Europe, while the USA was the dominant power in the west.

### The superpowers and Asia

At the end of the Second World War the USA was clearly the dominant power in Asia:

- The US Army had conquered Japan, and taken over the administration of much of the territory that had been occupied by Japan.
- The British and French Empires, which had once enjoyed considerable influence in south-east Asia, had been devastated by the War and were struggling to reassert themselves.
- China was unable to exercise much influence in the region as it was experiencing a civil war.
- The Soviet Union had only joined the war in Asia in mid-1945 and therefore occupied very little territory in the region.

> **East Asia and south-east Asia**
>
> It is important not to confuse East Asia with south-east Asia.
>
> East Asia refers to countries including Korea, Japan and China.
>
> South-east Asia refers to the countries south of China and east of India – this includes the countries now known as Malaya, Thailand, Laos, Cambodia and Vietnam.

### The division of Korea

Prior to the Second World War, Korea had been part of the Japanese Empire. As a result, in 1945, the USA and its ally the Soviet Union invaded Korea in the battle against Japan. Following their victory, they agreed to divide Korea at the **38th Parallel**. In 1948, **Stalin**, the leader of the Soviet Union, supported the creation of a communist government in the North of Korea, while Harry S. Truman, the **Democratic** US President, and the **United Nations (UN)** arranged free elections in the South.

## Complete the paragraph

Below are a sample exam-style question and a paragraph written in answer to this question. The paragraph contains a point and specific examples, but lacks a concluding explanatory link back to the question. Complete the paragraph adding this link in the space provided.

Why did the USA intervene in the Korean War?

> One reason why the USA intervened in the Korean War was superpower competition during the Cold War. For example, after the Second World War a rivalry developed between the USA and the Soviet Union. This rivalry was partly ideological and based on a clash between capitalist and communist systems. The US capitalist system was characterised by political democracy, individual rights, and a large amount of economic freedom. In contrast, the Soviet Union's communist system was dominated by a single political party, which restricted the political and economic freedom of its citizens. Both superpowers gained spheres of influence following the Second World War and the two rivals competed to protect and extend their geographical influence.
>
> _____
> _____
> _____
> _____
> _____
> _____
> _____

## Spot the mistake

Below are a sample exam-style question and a paragraph written in answer to this question. Why does this paragraph not get into Level 4? Once you have identified the mistake, rewrite the paragraph so that it displays the qualities of Level 4. The mark scheme on page 3 will help you.

Why did the USA intervene in the Korean War?

> During the Second World War, the USA and the Soviet Union were both part of the Grand Alliance and therefore were allies. After the defeat of the Axis Powers, tensions emerged in the relationship between the USA and the Soviet Union. One was capitalist and the other was communist. At the same time, the two powers became superpowers due to the collapse of the French Empire and the British Empire in East Asia. The USA had won the war over the Japanese Empire with very little help from the Soviet Union. Following this, the two powers agreed to divide Korea at the 38th Parallel. This led to the Korean War.

# Section 1: The Korean War, 1950–53: causes, course and consequences

## The causes of the Korean War: North Korean aggression

### Korea in 1949

| North Korea (DPRK) | South Korea (ROK) |
|---|---|
| Kim Il-Sung, the leader of the **Democratic People's Republic of Korea (DPRK)**, created a regime which was similar to Stalin's Russia:<br>• The government was dominated by the Communist Party.<br>• The secret police suppressed the communists' political enemies.<br>• The free market was replaced by a government-controlled economy. | Syngman Rhee was elected President of the **Republic of Korea (ROK)** in 1948. His government was established with US support, but the relationship became strained because the government was characterised by:<br>• authoritarianism: the repression of political opposition<br>• corruption<br>• collaboration with those who had supported Japan in the War. |

### Causes of the North Korean invasion

Kim was determined to reunite Korea under communist rule and sought Stalin's backing for an invasion. Initially, Stalin was unwilling to support military action. He was worried that if Russian and US troops met in battle, the conflict could escalate into a third world war. However, in April 1950, Kim travelled to Moscow and persuaded Stalin to back a communist invasion of South Korea.

### Communist China

In October 1949, following the Chinese Revolution, Mao Zedong had established the People's Republic of China (PRC) under a communist-dominated government. In February 1950 the Soviet Union and the PRC signed the Treaty of Friendship, Alliance and Mutual Assistance. These events were significant:

- The Soviet Union provided substantial military support to China, therefore establishing a powerful communist state in the region.
- Stalin expected China and North Korea to become allies. Consequently, Chinese troops, rather than Russian troops, could be used to support North Korea in the event of a war.
- In this way, Stalin believed that communist influence could be extended in East Asia, without risking direct conflict between the two superpowers.

#### US relations with China and Taiwan

Following the Chinese Revolution, the US government refused to recognise the new communist government of China. Rather, the USA recognised the former government of China as the official government. This government had fled to **Taiwan** after the communist revolution.

### The USA and Korea

At the same time, Stalin was not overly worried about US intervention in Korea for two reasons:

- In 1949, the Soviet Union successfully tested its first atomic bomb, gaining **nuclear parity** with the USA. Stalin believed this would prevent any conflict in Korea escalating into nuclear war. He believed that the USA would be deterred from launching a nuclear attack on the Soviet Union because the Soviet Union could now retaliate with nuclear weapons of its own.
- In January 1950, Dean Acheson, US Secretary of State, announced that Korea was not within the USA's **Pacific Defensive Perimeter**. Stalin believed that this meant North Korea could invade South Korea without provoking a response from the USA.

### The invasion

On 25 June 1950, Kim ordered the invasion of South Korea. Seven divisions of North Korean troops, equipped with Russian T-34 tanks, crossed the border heading for the capital of South Korea, Seoul. The invading force numbered 135,000 men, trained by the Russians.

Kim believed that victory would be swift as the South Korean army numbered only 95,000 men. These men were largely inexperienced in warfare and were poorly equipped for battle.

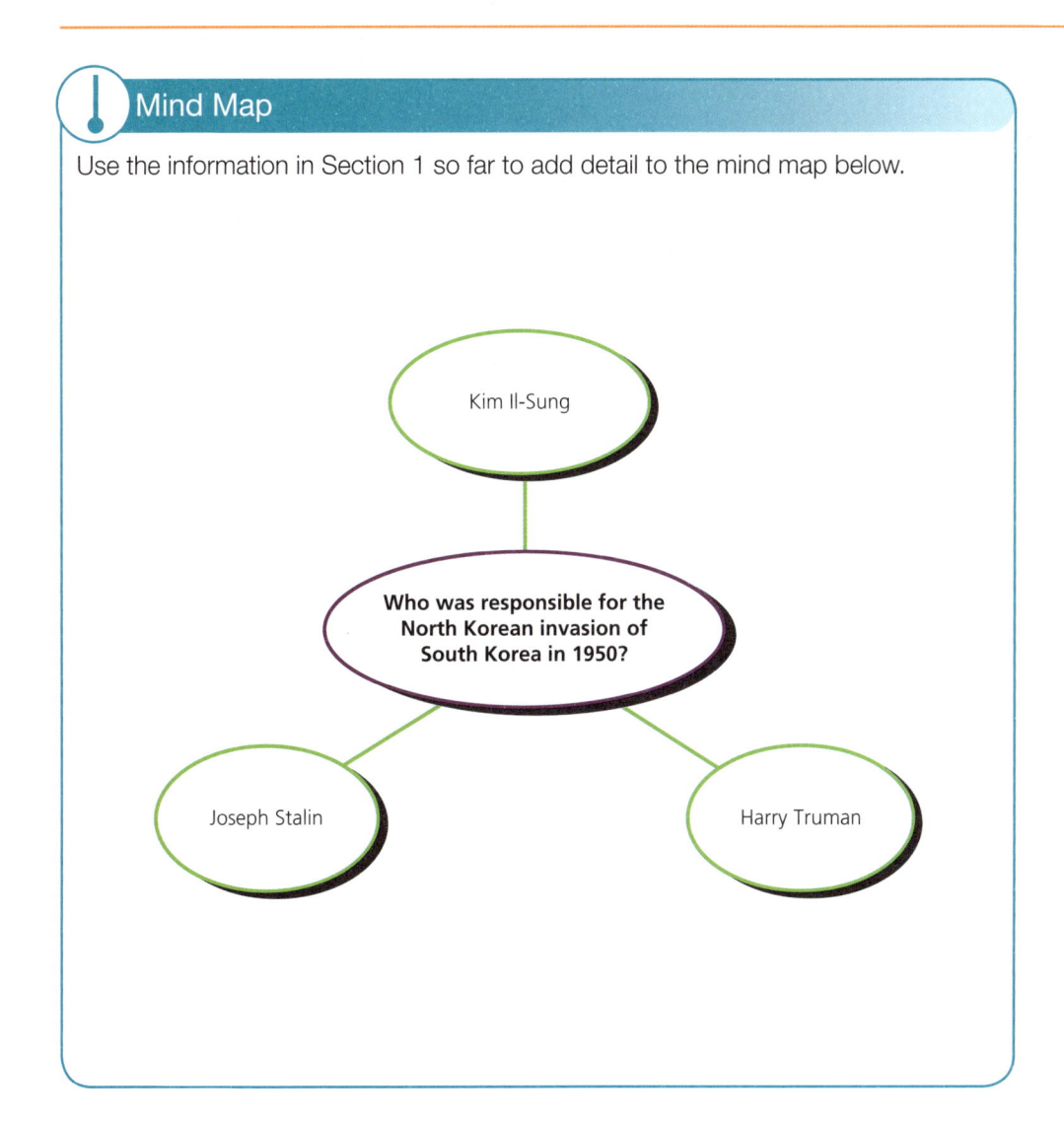

# Mind Map

Use the information in Section 1 so far to add detail to the mind map below.

- Kim Il-Sung
- **Who was responsible for the North Korean invasion of South Korea in 1950?**
  - Joseph Stalin
  - Harry Truman

# Spectrum of significance

Below are a sample exam-style question and a list of general points which could be used to answer the question. Use your own knowledge and the information on the opposite page to reach a judgement about the importance of these general points to the question posed. Write numbers on the spectrum below to indicate their relative importance. Then write a brief justification of your placement, explaining why some of these factors are more important than others. The resulting diagram could form the basis of an essay plan.

Why did North Korea invade South Korea in 1950?

1. The breakdown of the Grand Alliance
2. The division of Korea in 1945
3. Mao Zedong's revolution in China in 1949
4. Kim Il-Sung's meetings with Stalin in April 1950
5. US policy towards East Asia in 1950
6. Kim Il-Sung's desire to reunite Korea

Very important ⟵───────────────⟶ Less important

Section 1: The Korean War, 1950–53: causes, course and consequences

## The course of the Korean War, June–November 1950

Within two days of the North Korean attack, Truman had gained UN approval to defend South Korea. Truman chose to fight for the following reasons:

- Japan was the USA's key ally in East Asia. Truman believed that a united communist Korea, backed by China and Russia, would pose a threat to Japan.
- Truman was under pressure from the **China Lobby** to stand up to communism in Asia.
- The Truman Doctrine committed the USA to containing communism.
- It was easy for Truman to gain UN backing for an international force to defend South Korea as the USSR was boycotting the UN in protest at the US refusal to recognise communist China.

### The Truman Doctrine and NSC-68

Truman was not prepared to fight a third world war and defeat Stalin, but he wanted to contain communism, to prevent it spreading to other countries. Truman's commitment to 'containment' is known as the Truman Doctrine.

In April 1950, National Security Council resolution 68 (NSC-68) spelt out the costs of the Truman Doctrine. It argued that containment required a massive increase in US defence spending.

### United Nations Command (UNC)

On 7 July the United Nations created the United Nations Command led by the US General, **Douglas MacArthur**. Fifteen nations, including Britain, sent troops to fight as part of the UNC, but 90 per cent of the troops came from the USA and South Korea.

### The course of the War during 1950

#### North Korean advance

Initially, the North Korean forces were victorious. On 28 June 1950, they captured Seoul. Then they captured the whole of South Korea except for the UNC-controlled Pusan perimeter.

#### Counter-attack

The counter-attack began on 15 September, with the Inchon Landing, a surprise attack by UNC forces. The attack was extremely successful. Backed by overwhelming air power, UNC forces recaptured Seoul on 28 September. On 9 October, they crossed the 38th Parallel, invading North Korea.

#### Crossing the 38th Parallel

By 25 October, UNC forces approached North Korea's borders with China. Truman gave clear orders that MacArthur should stop at the Yalu River to avoid a confrontation with China. MacArthur ignored these orders and headed for the Chinese border on 24 November.

▼ A map showing the course of events in Korea, 1950–53.

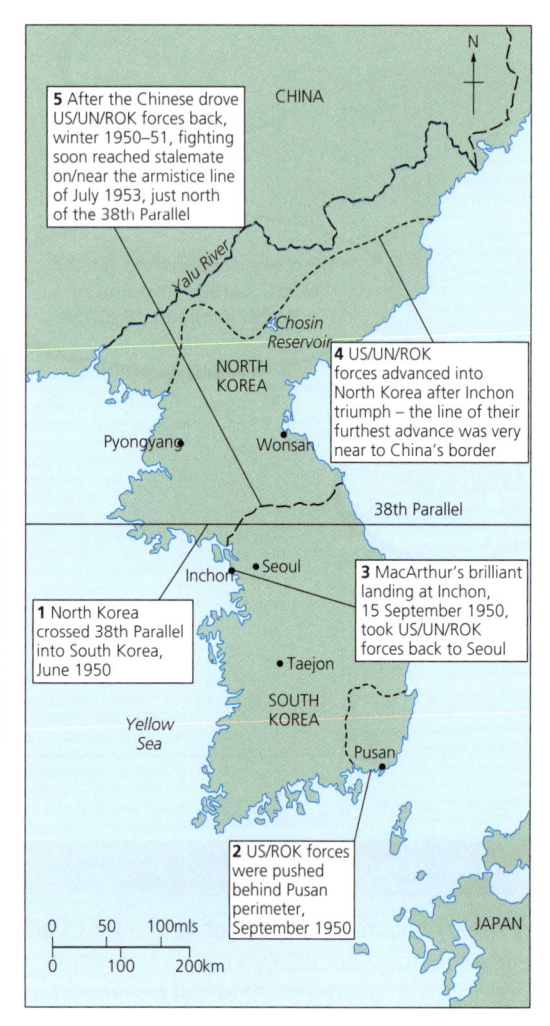

*[Map of Korea showing:]*
1. North Korea crossed 38th Parallel into South Korea, June 1950
2. US/ROK forces were pushed behind Pusan perimeter, September 1950
3. MacArthur's brilliant landing at Inchon, 15 September 1950, took US/UN/ROK forces back to Seoul
4. US/UN/ROK forces advanced into North Korea after Inchon triumph – the line of their furthest advance was very near to China's border
5. After the Chinese drove US/UN/ROK forces back, winter 1950–51, fighting soon reached stalemate on/near the armistice line of July 1953, just north of the 38th Parallel

### From containment to rollback

Crossing the 38th Parallel went beyond containment. The new mission of the UN forces was to 'roll back' communism. Truman authorised the new policy of **rollback** because he:

- wanted to win support for the US **Congressional elections** in November. The war was popular as 64 per cent of the public backed the fight against communism
- was under pressure from Rhee to reunite Korea under his rule
- was ideologically committed to the fight against communism
- was keen to end the war swiftly with a complete victory over North Korea
- assumed that Stalin would not intervene for fear of causing a nuclear war.

## Support or challenge?

Below is a sample exam-style question which asks how far you agree with a specific statement. Below this are a series of general statements which are relevant to the question. Using your own knowledge and the information on the opposite page, decide whether these statements support or challenge the statement in the question and tick the appropriate box.

'America's strategy in Korea was highly successful from June to November 1950.' How far do you agree with this statement?

| Statement | SUPPORT | CHALLENGE |
| --- | --- | --- |
| MacArthur launched the Inchon Landing on 15 September. | | |
| Truman obtained UN backing for an invasion of Korea. | | |
| North Korean troops captured Seoul at the end of June. | | |
| UNC forces began to 'roll back' communism in October. | | |
| The UNC was formed under the leadership of General Douglas MacArthur. | | |
| UNC forces recaptured Seoul on 28 September. | | |
| The UNC maintained control of the Pusan perimeter in June 1950. | | |
| UNC forces approached the Chinese border in November. | | |

## Eliminate irrelevance

Below are a sample exam-style question and a paragraph written in answer to this question. Read the paragraph and identify parts of the paragraph that are not directly relevant to the question. Draw a line through the information that is irrelevant and justify your deletions in the margin.

How far do you agree that Truman's main reason for becoming involved in the Korean War in 1950 was to contain communist aggression?

> One reason why Truman became involved in the Korean War in 1950 was to contain communism in East Asia. Truman knew that the North Korean invasion had communist Russia's backing. Truman was committed to standing up to communism, a policy known as 'containment'. Also, the Republic of Korea, also known as South Korea, was struggling due to Syngman Rhee's government, which was corrupt and repressive. Additionally, Truman had been criticised by the China Lobby for 'losing China' to communism in 1949. Therefore, he was under pressure to act strongly in East Asia to resist the spread of communism. Communists believed that single-party government was better than political democracy and that the government should control the economy. In this way, Truman became involved in the Korean War because he was committed to preventing the spread of communism.

Section 1: The Korean War, 1950–53: causes, course and consequences

## The course of the Korean War, November 1950–April 1951

### Why China intervened

With UNC troops approaching the Chinese border, and North Korean forces in retreat, Mao Zedong was under intense pressure to intervene in support of North Korea:

- He was worried UN forces would conquer North Korea and invade China.
- Stalin put pressure on him to enter the war.
- He anticipated Russian aid under the terms of the Treaty of Friendship (see page 6).
- He believed that a successful war against the USA would make his regime more popular in China, consolidating his power.
- He knew that China could intervene without formally declaring war on the USA by sending an army of volunteers rather than China's official army. This would ensure that the war would not escalate into a confrontation between the USA and China.

### The course of the war: winter 1950–51

#### Chinese intervention

On 26 November 1950, 200,000 volunteer Chinese troops entered the war to support the North Korean troops. The Soviet Union provided limited air support behind enemy lines. Chinese and North Korean soldiers advanced quickly and on 4 January 1951 captured Seoul.

#### UN counter-attack

In mid-January 1951, the USA launched a massive counter-attack. After intense fighting, UNC forces recaptured Seoul on 15 March.

### The consequences of Chinese intervention: stalemate

Following the recapture of Seoul, the war entered a phase of stalemate in which neither side had an obvious advantage. The stalemate came about for the following reasons:

- The scale of Chinese forces balanced the better equipped UN forces, making a military breakthrough on either side difficult.
- Stalin wanted to continue the war because:
  - it kept the USA distracted
  - it was making relations between Britain and the USA difficult
  - it made China more dependent on the USSR.
- Additionally, he knew that Truman had ruled out the use of nuclear weapons and that the risk of the conflict escalating into a war between the superpowers was very low.
- Truman, on the other hand, wished to end the war as it was expensive and had become unpopular in the USA. However, neither option for ending the war was practical:
  - Truman was considering breaking the stalemate using nuclear weapons but the British Prime Minister, Clement Attlee, refused to support this, threatening to pull British troops out of Korea if nuclear weapons were deployed.
  - Stalin was unwilling to negotiate and Truman could not negotiate directly with Mao Zedong because the USA refused to recognise communist China.

### The sacking of MacArthur

On 11 April 1951, Truman fired General MacArthur, the leader of the UNC forces in Korea:

- Truman and MacArthur disagreed on the appropriate strategy for ending the war. Truman favoured a ceasefire and a return to a divided Korea. MacArthur wanted to use nuclear weapons, regardless of British objections, and invade North Korea and possibly China.
- Truman was aware that MacArthur ignored direct orders. For example, MacArthur deliberately ignored the order not to advance to the Chinese border.
- MacArthur had used the media to express disagreement with Truman's strategy.
- Truman believed that MacArthur's willingness to take risks in battle could lead to an escalation of the conflict and a third world war.
- After the intervention of the Chinese, MacArthur had failed to make a decisive impact on the war.

## RAG – Rate the timeline

Below are a sample exam-style question and a timeline. Read the question, study the timeline and, using three coloured pens, put a red, amber or green star next to the events to show:

- red – events and policies that have no relevance to the question
- amber – events and policies that have some significance to the question
- green – events and policies that are directly relevant to the question.

1. How far do you agree that the American government pursued a consistent policy in Korea in the period 1950–53?

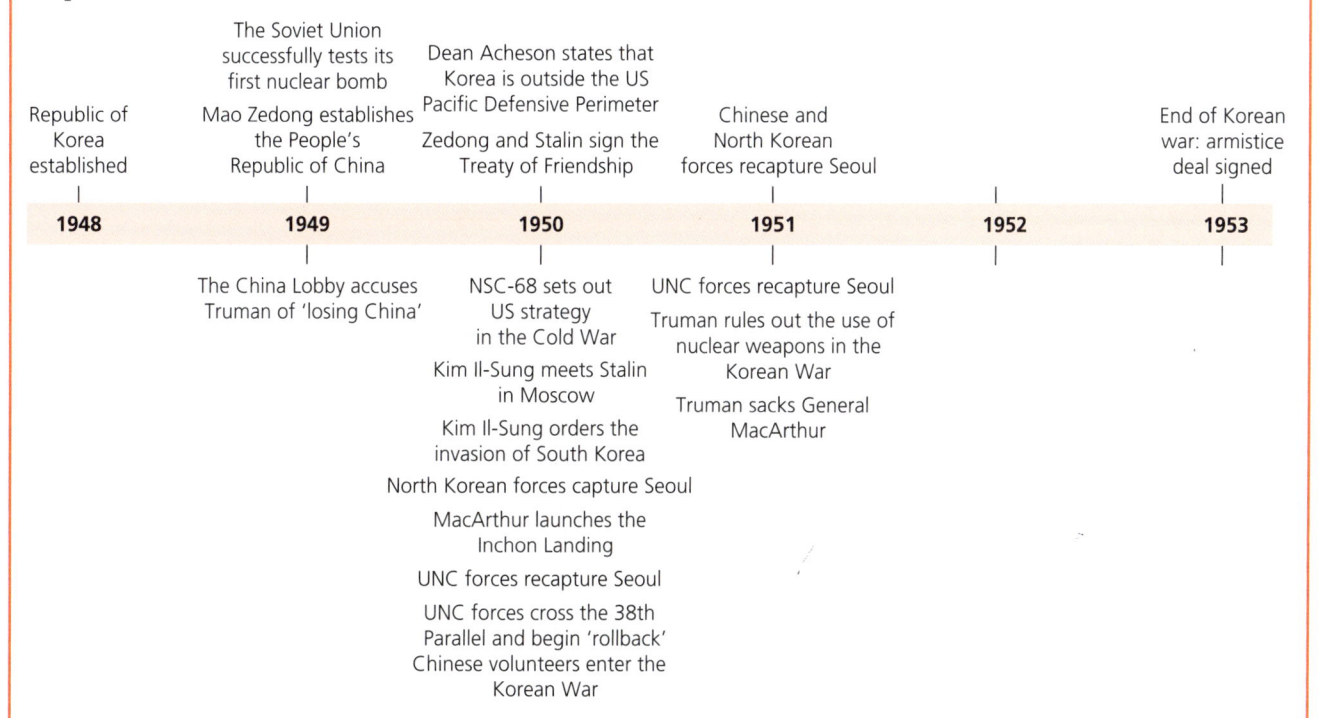

**Above the timeline:**

- **1948:** Republic of Korea established
- **1949:** The Soviet Union successfully tests its first nuclear bomb; Mao Zedong establishes the People's Republic of China
- **1950:** Dean Acheson states that Korea is outside the US Pacific Defensive Perimeter; Zedong and Stalin sign the Treaty of Friendship
- **1951:** Chinese and North Korean forces recapture Seoul
- **1953:** End of Korean war: armistice deal signed

**Below the timeline:**

- **1949:** The China Lobby accuses Truman of 'losing China'
- **1950:** NSC-68 sets out US strategy in the Cold War; Kim Il-Sung meets Stalin in Moscow; Kim Il-Sung orders the invasion of South Korea; North Korean forces capture Seoul; MacArthur launches the Inchon Landing; UNC forces recapture Seoul; UNC forces cross the 38th Parallel and begin 'rollback'; Chinese volunteers enter the Korean War
- **1951:** UNC forces recapture Seoul; Truman rules out the use of nuclear weapons in the Korean War; Truman sacks General MacArthur

Now repeat the activity with the following questions. You could use different colours, or number your stars 1, 2 and 3.

2. How far do you agree that China's involvement in the Korean War was the main reason why a stalemate developed in 1951–53?
3. Why did Truman sack General MacArthur in 1951?

## Develop the detail (a)

Below are a sample exam-style question and a paragraph written in answer to this question. The paragraph contains a limited amount of detail. Annotate the paragraph to add additional detail to the answer.

Why did the Korean War develop into a stalemate in 1951?

> One reason why the Korean War developed into a stalemate in 1951 was the entry of China into the war. Chinese troops entered the Korean War to support the communists. They were helped by the Soviet Union. The number of Chinese troops helped to balance the strength of the opposing forces, and the Chinese soldiers advanced quickly. In this way, China's entry into the Korean War contributed to the stalemate as it increased the forces opposing the UNC troops.

**Section 1:** The Korean War, 1950–53: causes, course and consequences

## Armistice negotiations

### Why were armistice negotiations protracted?

By mid-1951, the war was placing a great strain on the resources of both China and the USA. Mao Zedong had anticipated generous help from the Soviet Union. However, Stalin made Zedong pay in full for the equipment supplied by the Soviet Union.

It was in the interests of both sides to end the war, and negotiations began in July 1951. Nonetheless, armistice negotiations were difficult. Firstly, none of the major powers was enthusiastic about a peace deal:

- Neither China nor the USA was prepared to back down.
- Stalin wanted the war to continue (see page 10) and therefore did nothing to encourage negotiations.
- The USA was experiencing a 'Red Scare', which meant that Truman was under pressure to make no concessions to communism.

> **The Red Scare**
>
> Between 1947 and 1953, the USA experienced a 'Red Scare'. Democratic senator Joseph McCarthy argued that the US government had been penetrated by Soviet spies. He argued that Truman's government was doing too little to counter the threat of communism at home and abroad. Evidence of a communist spy ring emerged in the late 1940s as Julius and Ethel Rosenberg were convicted for passing the USA's nuclear secrets to the Soviet Union. The trial started in March 1951, at the very time that Truman was first considering a deal with North Korea.

Secondly, there were key issues which proved difficult to resolve. The border between North and South Korea was contentious. Territory had changed hands during the war and both sides were keen to gain some land as a result of the negotiations. Therefore, neither side was eager to re-establish the 38th Parallel as the dividing line between the two Koreas.

Another important issue related to prisoners of war. The USA argued that prisoners of war should not be **repatriated** against their will. However, China and North Korea wanted all prisoners of war to be repatriated regardless of their preference.

Finally, the USA refused to recognise communist China. Consequently, US and Chinese diplomats never negotiated directly with each other.

### Successful negotiations

A peace deal was finally agreed on 27 July 1953. The armistice deal, which was signed at Pan Mun Jon, was brought about for the following reasons:

- Stalin had died in March 1953. The new Soviet leadership was keen to improve relations with the USA and in this way to ease Cold War tensions. Therefore, they put pressure on China and North Korea to make concessions.
- Dwight D. Eisenhower, who became **Republican** President in January 1953, put pressure on Syngman Rhee to agree to a ceasefire in return for continued US military and financial support.
- China and North Korea were concerned that Eisenhower would use nuclear weapons against them.
- The war was placing an enormous strain on the Chinese economy.

The **armistice** agreed:

- a new border between North and South Korea
- the creation of the Korean **Demilitarised Zone (DMZ)** along the border, which would be policed by both sides and the UN
- that peace talks would continue between all parties.

## Simple essay style

Below is a sample exam-style question. Use your own knowledge and the information on the opposite page to produce a plan for this question. Choose four general points, and provide three pieces of specific information to support each general point. Once you have planned your essay, write the introduction and conclusion for the essay. The introduction should list the points to be discussed in the essay. The conclusion should summarise the key points and justify which point was the most important.

Why were armistice negotiations at the end of the Korean War so protracted?

## Identify an argument

Below are a series of definitions, a sample exam-style question and two sample conclusions. One of the conclusions achieves a high level because it contains an argument. The other achieves a lower level because it contains only description and assertion. Identify which is which. The mark scheme on page 3 will help you.

- Description: a detailed account.
- Assertion: a statement of fact or an opinion which is not supported by a reason.
- Reason: a statement which explains or justifies something.
- Argument: an assertion justified with a reason.

How far do you agree that Stalin's unwillingness to end the war was the main reason why armistice negotiations were so protracted?

### Sample 1

In conclusion, Stalin had a clear interest in prolonging the war and so was unwilling to end it. He knew that the war was costing America, his Cold War rival, greatly. He also knew that as the war dragged on, Mao Zedong was becoming more and more dependent on the Soviet Union for aid. Therefore, it was in his interests to prolong the war rather than appealing to Truman and Zedong to reach a settlement.

### Sample 2

In conclusion, there were four reasons why armistice negotiations were so protracted. Firstly, neither China nor the USA was willing to back down. Secondly, Stalin was unwilling to end the war. Thirdly, Truman did not want to be seen as 'soft on communism'. Finally, there were disagreements over issues such as prisoners of war and the exact border between the two Koreas.

Section 1: The Korean War, 1950–53: causes, course and consequences

# The impact of the Korean War

Revised

## How successful was the USA?

| US Successes | Explanation |
|---|---|
| • US action had maintained the independence of South Korea. | • Without US support, South Korea would have been overrun in the first phase of the war. |
| • The threat of communism in Asia led to the creation of SEATO in 1954. | • SEATO, the South-East Asia Treaty Organisation, united Britain, France, Japan, the Philippines, Australia, New Zealand, South Korea, Pakistan, Thailand, and the USA in a common pact to defend each other against communism. |
| • The war consolidated the USA's relationship with Japan. | • During the war, the USA spent $3 billion on Japanese weapons, boosting the Japanese economy and stimulating a trading relationship between the two countries.<br>• The USA and Japan signed a security treaty in September 1951 allowing US troops to be stationed in Japan to protect Japan against Russia and China. |
| • The US avoided direct conflict with the Soviet Union. | • Truman had assumed that Stalin would enter the war in support of North Korea. However, he knew that Stalin would be unwilling to enter the war against the UN as the UN was a respected international body. |

| US Failures | Explanation |
|---|---|
| • UN forces had failed to 'roll back' communism. | • MacArthur's forces were unable to consolidate the gains made in North Korea. Indeed, the armistice agreement reasserted the original border at the 38th Parallel. |
| • Truman was unable to use nuclear weapons to end the war. | • Truman was forced to submit to international pressure not to use nuclear weapons and this demonstrated the limits of his power. |
| • The USA was humiliated by the Chinese army. | • UNC troops were better trained and better equipped than the Chinese army. Nonetheless, Chinese intervention had forced US-led troops out of North Korea. |
| • The war had been very costly for the USA. | • In economic terms, the USA was forced to increase defence spending from 4 per cent of **GNP** in 1948 to 14 per cent of GNP in 1953.<br>• In human terms, the war led to the deaths of 33,000 US soldiers. |
| • The US public had become increasingly reluctant to support the war. | • During 1952, the war became increasingly unpopular with the US public. This indicated that the US public were no longer committed to the fight against communism. |

Overall, Truman's policy of containment had been successful. Nonetheless, Truman's political enemies argued that containment was not enough and that Truman had failed to fulfil his promise to 'roll back' communism in Korea.

## The impact of the Korean War on Asia

### Korea

The war cost Korea greatly. It led to the deaths of around 10 per cent of the Korean population. It also led to massive economic damage, destroying around 600,000 homes and 8,700 factories. In addition, neither Rhee nor Kim Il-Sung had succeeded in their long-term goal of reuniting Korea.

### China

Over 150,000 Chinese troops were killed. Additionally, the war diverted Mao Zedong's attention from conquering Taiwan. In this sense, the war stopped Mao achieving his long-term foreign policy goal. The war exposed weaknesses in the Chinese army, and therefore led to costly military reform. Nonetheless, the Korean War helped Zedong to consolidate his power in China because he had successfully stood up to the USA.

### Turning assertion into argument

Below are a sample exam-style question and a series of assertions. Read the question and then add a justification to each of the assertions to turn it into an argument.

How far do you agree that neither the United States nor China achieved success in the Korean War?

> The USA was successful in the Korean War in the sense that
> ___
> ___

> The USA was unsuccessful in the Korean War in the sense that
> ___
> ___

> China was partially successful in the Korean War in the sense that
> ___
> ___

### You're the examiner

Below are a sample exam-style question and a paragraph written in answer to this question. Read the paragraph and the mark scheme provided on page 3. Decide which level you would award the paragraph. Write the level below, along with a justification for your choice.

How successful was the USA's intervention in the Korean War?

> One way in which US intervention in Korea was successful was that it stopped the spread of communism in East Asia. At first, the North was successful, and then UNC troops fought back. Finally, a stalemate developed after Chinese volunteers entered the war. At the end of the war, an armistice was agreed which officially divided Korea between communists in the North and capitalists in the South. In this way, the USA did not destroy communism in Korea, but it did prevent it from spreading from North Korea to South Korea.
>
> Level:    Reason for choosing this level:
> ___
> ___

### Recommended reading

Below is a list of suggested further reading on this topic.

- Vivienne Sanders, *Access to History: The USA in Asia 1945–1975* (pages 9–78). Hodder Education, 2010.
- Martin McCauley, *Russia, America and the Cold War, 1949–91* (pages 36–42). Longman, 2004.
- John W. Young and John Kent, *International Relations Since 1945: A Global History* (pages 146–152). Oxford University Press, 2004.

**Section 1:** The Korean War, 1950–53: causes, course and consequences

## Exam focus

Below is a sample A-grade essay. Read it and the examiner's comments around it.

> How far do you agree that Truman's desire to contain communism was the main reason why the United States became so deeply involved in the Korean War in the years 1950–53?

Truman's desire to contain communism was clearly the main reason for the United States' initial involvement in the Korean War. However, it does not explain the deepening involvement of the USA in Korea. Instead, this is explained by US domestic politics, the involvement of the UN, and China's entry into the war. These factors created a situation in which Truman could neither win nor back down and therefore Truman was forced to extend and deepen his involvement in the war.

Truman's commitment to 'contain' communism was the main reason why the USA became so deeply involved in the Korean War. Containment, or the Truman Doctrine, describes Truman's willingness to commit US resources to stop communism spreading beyond the sphere of influence established by Stalin at the end of the Second World War. The North Korean invasion of South Korea in June 1950 was the first military test of containment. Truman's commitment to containment meant that he was unwilling to allow the communists to conquer South Korea. Consequently, Truman sent US troops to defend South Korea as part of a UN force. In this way, Truman's commitment to containing communism explains the initial involvement of the USA as Truman wanted to stop the spread of communism in Korea.

US involvement in Korea is also explained by the Cold War context. Truman believed that the USA was involved in an ideological and military struggle with the Soviet Union. The USA stood for democracy and capitalism, whereas the Soviet Union was based on a single-party dictatorship and a socialist economy in which the government controlled all economic resources. For Truman, the influence of the Soviet Union was a threat to the USA because it challenged freedom and democracy — the US way of life. In this way, the Cold War context explains Truman's decision to send US troops to Korea in the sense that it explains Truman's commitment to containment. Truman was committed to protecting freedom by containing communism in East Asia.

Following Truman's decision to send troops to Korea, US domestic politics put pressure on Truman to deepen his involvement. Truman was under pressure from the China Lobby following the communist revolution in China in 1949. The China Lobby blamed Truman for 'losing China' to communism. At the same time, Truman was under pressure from Senator Joseph McCarthy, who had accused Truman of failing to root

*Examiner's comments:*

- This is a focused introduction that outlines the structure of the rest of the essay, and states the overall argument that containment explains initial involvement, but other factors explain the deepening involvement of the USA.

- The essay uses dates to illustrate its points. This shows depth of knowledge which enables the essay to achieve highly within the level awarded.

- This paragraph draws links between its own point and that of the previous paragraph. This contributes to the overall argument of the essay.

- This paragraph addresses the specific focus of the question by directly considering the USA's deepening involvement in the Korean War.

out communists from his government. Pressure from the China Lobby and Joseph McCarthy meant that Truman could not afford to be seen as 'soft on communism'. Therefore, following the crossing of the 38th Parallel, Truman deepened US involvement in Korea, developing his policy from containment to 'rollback'.

Another reason for the deepening involvement of the USA in Korea was the backing of the UN. Truman sought UN backing for his intervention in Korea because the UN was a respected international body and the involvement of the UN would legitimise US involvement in Korea. The UNC force was headed by the US General Douglas MacArthur, and included forces from fifteen nations. The involvement of the UN allowed the USA to deepen its involvement in Korea because it gave the USA international support for the fight against communism.

China's entry into the Korean War also deepened US involvement in the Korean War. Chinese forces entered the war in November 1950. The 200,000 Chinese volunteers helped to balance the strength of the opposing forces. Therefore Chinese involvement created a stalemate which lasted for another two and a half years. China's entry forced Truman to prolong US involvement in the Korean War because the USA no longer had military advantage over the opposing forces and therefore a decisive victory was impossible. In this way, China's entry into the War deepened US involvement because it created a stalemate, forcing the USA to remain involved in Korea for two and a half years.

*This paragraph deals with the period from 1950 to 1953, ensuring that the essay covers the whole time period specified in the question.*

In conclusion, Truman's commitment to containment explains initial US involvement in the Korean War, but the deepening involvement is best explained by US domestic policy which made it politically impossible for Truman to back down, China's entry into the war which meant that the US could not win a clear victory, and UN involvement which meant that the USA had international authority to continue fighting.

*The conclusion shows the way that the different factors combined, explaining both the initial and deepening involvement of the USA in Korea.*

30/30
This is a Level 5 essay due to the fact that it has a clear argument that is sustained throughout the essay. This argument contrasts reasons for initial involvement with reasons for deepening involvement and therefore explicitly addresses the question. The essay achieves a high mark in Level 5 due to the fact that the argument is supported by a good range and depth of detailed knowledge.

### Reverse engineering

The best essays are based on careful plans. Read the essay and the examiner's comments and try to work out the general points of the plan used to write the essay. Once you have done this, note down the specific examples used to support each general point.

# Section 2:
# The ideological struggle in south-east Asia in the early 1950s

## Imperial decline in south-east Asia

During the nineteenth century, the British and French empires established control over most of south-east Asia. Britain controlled Burma and Malaya, while France controlled Indochina, the region that later became Laos, Cambodia and Vietnam. The two powers agreed that Thailand would remain independent and act as a **buffer zone** between the two empires.

▼ A map showing south-east Asia in 1950.

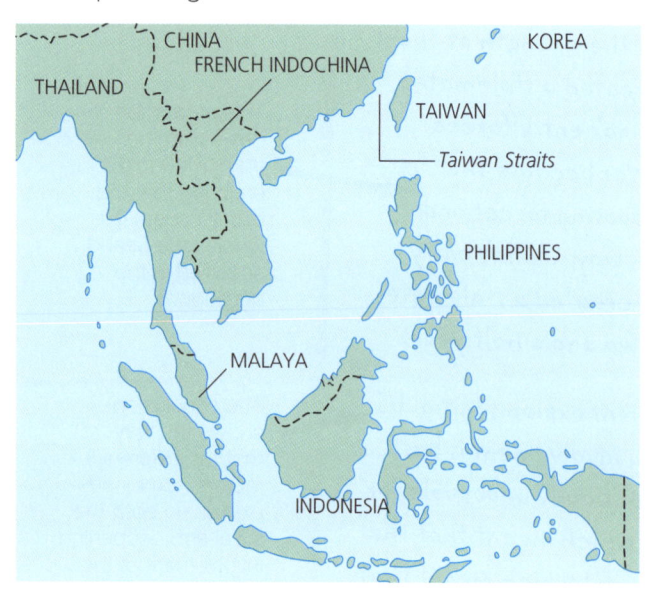

In 1941 and 1942, the Japanese empire conquered the British and French territory. Following the war, Britain and France attempted to reassert their control of the region. However, this proved difficult due to the emergence of **nationalist** and communist movements, dedicated to fighting for independence from these empires.

### French Indochina, 1945–50

Following the Second World War, the French struggled to regain control in Indochina. Their hardest task was reasserting control over Vietnam:

- They faced a **guerrilla** force called the **Viet Minh** led by Ho Chi Minh. Ho was both a nationalist and a communist. The Viet Minh's guerrilla tactics were extremely successful.
- France, which had been devastated by the Second World War, could not afford to sustain a conflict in the area.
- Successive French governments changed their policy regarding the region and therefore their approach to the Viet Minh was inconsistent.

### British Malaya

In 1948, the Malayan communist movement began fighting the British in order to gain independence. The Malayan National Liberation Army, led by Chin Peng, was a pro-Chinese movement, supported by the minority ethnic Chinese community in Malaya but not supported by the majority ethnic Malayan population. The British fought back and, under the leadership of General Sir Harold Briggs, were able to maintain control of the region. However, retaining control was a continual struggle and the **Malayan Emergency** lasted until 1960.

### US reaction to the growth of communism in south-east Asia

The US government was extremely concerned about the events in south-east Asia. It believed that communism would emerge victorious following imperial decline. US fears were heightened by the establishment of a communist regime in China in 1949, and the communist invasion of South Korea in 1950 (see page 6). Truman was particularly concerned by the failure of the French to reassert control in Vietnam. Consequently, as part of his policy of containment, Truman began to provide support for the French in their fight against communism in the region.

## Mind Map

Use the information on the opposite page to add detail to the mind map below.

- **The context of USA policy in south-east Asia**
  - The growth of nationalism in south-east Asia
  - The problems faced by European powers in south-east Asia
  - The spread of communism in Asia, 1949–50

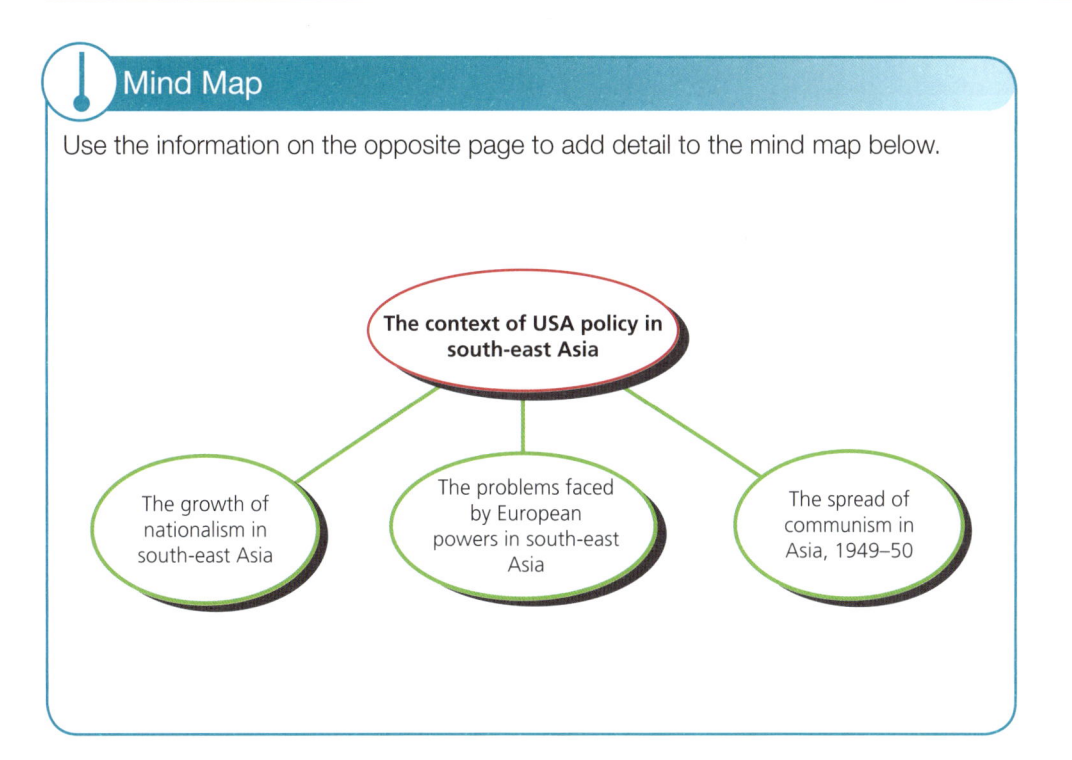

## Eliminate irrelevance

Below are a sample exam-style question and a paragraph written in answer to this question. Read the paragraph and identify parts of the paragraph that are not directly relevant to the question. Draw a line through the information that is irrelevant and justify your deletions in the margin.

How far do you agree that the decline of imperialism in south-east Asia was the main reason for US intervention in the region between 1950 and 1954?

> One reason for US intervention in south-east Asia between 1950 and 1954 was the decline of imperialism in the region. For example, the Japanese Empire had lost control of Korea at the end of the Second World War. Following the Second World War, Ho Chi Minh and the Viet Minh were extremely successful in waging a guerrilla war against the French Empire. Similarly, the British Empire was under threat from Chin Peng's Malayan National Liberation Army in Malaya. Britain and the USA had both been part of the Grand Alliance, along with the Soviet Union, during the Second World War. Both the Viet Minh and the MNLA were communist, and their struggle for national liberation led to an increase in their support. In this way, the decline of imperialism led to US intervention in south-east Asia because the USA feared that the struggle against imperialism was leading to the growth of communism in south-east Asia.

**Section 2:** The ideological struggle in south-east Asia in the early 1950s

## US involvement in south-east Asia, 1950–54

At the end of the Second World War, Truman agreed that France should regain its territory in Indochina. Nonetheless, the Viet Minh declared the independence of Vietnam in September 1945, creating the Democratic Republic of Vietnam (DRV). They established an independent capital in Hanoi, in the North of Vietnam. The French government refused to surrender Vietnam and set up a rival capital in Saigon, in southern Vietnam.

### The reasons for US help to the French

Truman decided to help the French for the following reasons:

- Truman needed French support in Europe as part of the Cold War struggle against the Soviet Union. He hoped that the French would support him in Europe in return for US support in Vietnam.
- Truman believed that Ho Chi Minh was a 'Soviet puppet' who was trying to establish Vietnam as a Russian **satellite state**.
- The **China Lobby** and Senator Joseph McCarthy were putting pressure on Truman to stand up to communism.
- Truman believed that communism was a growing problem in south-east Asia and while he trusted the British to deal with it effectively in Malaya, he did not trust the French to reassert control over Vietnam.

### US intervention in Vietnam, 1950–52

Truman offered the French financial help and military advisors.

- In May 1950, Truman authorised an initial payment of $10 million to the French administration in Vietnam.
- By the end of 1950, Truman had sent $100 million in addition to military equipment including aircraft, **Napalm** and patrol boats.
- By 1952, the USA was paying 80 per cent of France's war costs. This amounted to $2 billion per year.

### Viet Minh successes, 1952–54

In spite of US support, the French were unable to suppress the Viet Minh. Indeed, in the period 1952–54, the Viet Minh consolidated their control of much of northern Vietnam. The Viet Minh were successful for the following reasons:

- By 1952, the Viet Minh had 250,000 soldiers and a **militia** which numbered 2 million.
- Between 1950 and 1952, the Chinese provided weapons to the Viet Minh.
- The majority of the population in northern Vietnam supported the struggle for independence and therefore supported the Viet Minh.
- The Viet Minh had a greater understanding than the French of the geography of Vietnam.
- The French army were not equipped or trained to counter the Viet Minh's guerrilla tactics.
- The Viet Minh were led by an experienced and successful general, Vo Nguyen Giap.

### The US response

**Republicans** and **Democrats** were united in the belief that south-east Asia was of great importance to the USA's interests. Both parties were convinced that the loss of any part of south-east Asia to communism must be avoided at all costs. Therefore, Truman continued support for the French. South-east Asia played a major role in the US Presidential election of 1952. Republican candidate Eisenhower criticised Truman's policy of containment in the region, arguing that it was immoral merely to contain the communist enemy. Eisenhower called for the policy of **rollback** – temporarily endorsed by Truman during the Korean War – to be adopted as the defining feature of US policy in south-east Asia. Eisenhower's tough stance on the Cold War was an important factor in his victory in the election.

## Complete the paragraph

Below are a sample exam-style question and a paragraph written in answer to this question. The paragraph contains a point and specific examples, but lacks a concluding explanatory link back to the question. Complete the paragraph adding this link in the space provided.

Why did the USA become increasingly involved in south-east Asia in the period 1950–54?

> One reason why the USA became increasingly involved in south-east Asia in the period 1950–54 was the influence of the China Lobby. For example,
>
> _____
> _____
> _____
> _____
>
> In this way, the influence of the China Lobby led to increasing US involvement because it forced Truman to take a firm stand against communism in Asia.

## Spectrum of significance

Below are a sample exam-style question and a list of general points which could be used to answer the question. Use your own knowledge and the information on the opposite page to reach a judgement about the importance of these general points to the question posed. Write numbers on the spectrum below to indicate their relative importance. Having done this, write a brief justification of your placement, explaining why some of these factors are more important than others. The resulting diagram could form the basis of an essay plan.

Why did the USA become increasingly involved in south-east Asia in the period 1950–54?

1. The China Lobby
2. The Truman Doctrine
3. The decline of imperial power in south-east Asia
4. Truman believed that Ho Chi Minh was heavily influenced by Stalin
5. The establishment of the Democratic Republic of Vietnam in 1945
6. Viet Minh successes in the period 1952–54

Very important ←――――――――――――――――――→ Less important

Section 2: The ideological struggle in south-east Asia in the early 1950s

# The Geneva Peace Conference, 1954

Revised

## Dien Bien Phu

In 1954, the French, backed by the USA, built a fort in northern Vietnam. The fort of Dien Bien Phu was designed to hold 12,000 French soldiers, to cut off supplies from China, and to force the Viet Minh into a **pitched battle** that they were bound to lose because of the superiority of French **conventional forces**.

However, the Viet Minh attacked Dien Bien Phu from the hills and Giap's forces, combined with local peasants, defeated the French forces and took the fort.

The failure of Dien Bien Phu played a role in forcing the French to negotiate for peace. Moreover, the Soviet leadership and China had signalled their willingness to back peace talks. Indeed, both China and Russia put pressure on Ho Chi Minh to negotiate.

## The Geneva Conference

The Geneva Conference started on 8 May 1954, one day after the fall of Dien Bien Phu. Representatives from France and China, alongside nationalists from Vietnam, Cambodia and Laos, attended the conference, which was chaired by Britain and the Soviet Union.

### US hopes for the conference

The USA did not send representatives to the conference as it continued to refuse to recognise communist China. Nonetheless, it put pressure on its **NATO** allies to achieve the following goals:

- to stop the spread of communism in south-east Asia
- to prevent another war in Asia – the USA had no desire to be involved in another costly war in the region
- to establish a prosperous, independent, non-communist Vietnam.

### Peace negotiations

Ho Chi Minh was in a very strong position due to the military success of the Viet Minh. Nonetheless, under pressure from the Soviet Union and China he made a series of concessions. As a result, the conference agreed the Geneva Accords.

### The Geneva Accords

The participants at the conference agreed:

- an immediate end to hostilities
- the temporary division of Vietnam at the **17th Parallel**. The Viet Minh would control northern Vietnam, while the French would control southern Vietnam
- to create a **Demilitarised Zone (DMZ)** around the 17th Parallel to prevent conflict between the North and the South
- France would withdraw from southern Vietnam by 1956
- Vietnam would be reunited in 1956 and governed by a democratically elected government
- Laos and Cambodia would become independent and remain neutral (allied to neither the USA nor the Soviet Union)
- all foreign troops would be withdrawn from Vietnam, Laos and Cambodia.

▼ A map of divided Vietnam.

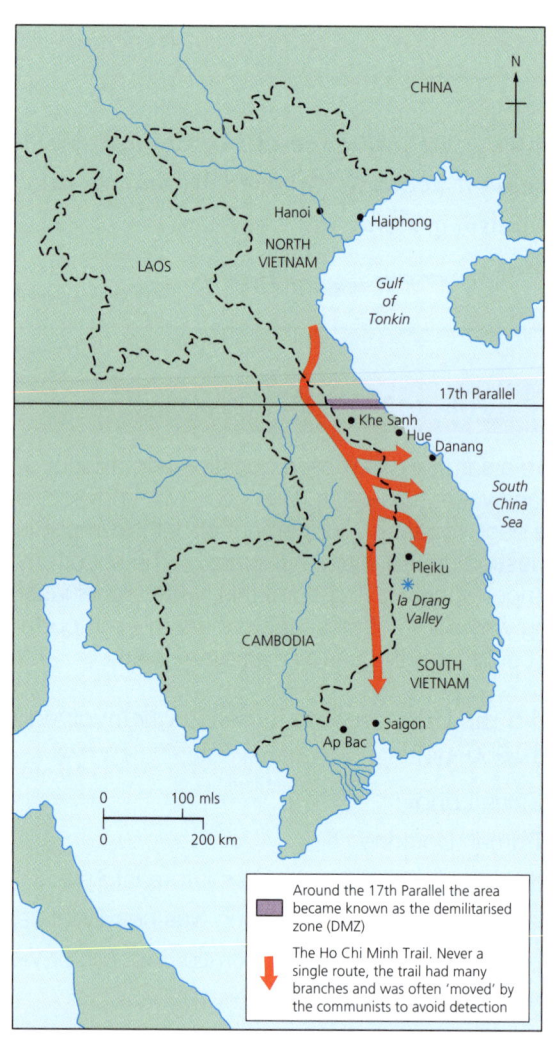

## Ho Chi Minh's reasons for agreeing to the Accords

Ho Chi Minh agreed to future democratic elections because he believed that he had overwhelming support in the North and enough support in the South to ensure a Viet Minh victory. Minh anticipated reuniting Vietnam in 1956 under his leadership.

# Mind Map

Use the information in Sections 1 and 2 so far to add detail to the mind map below.

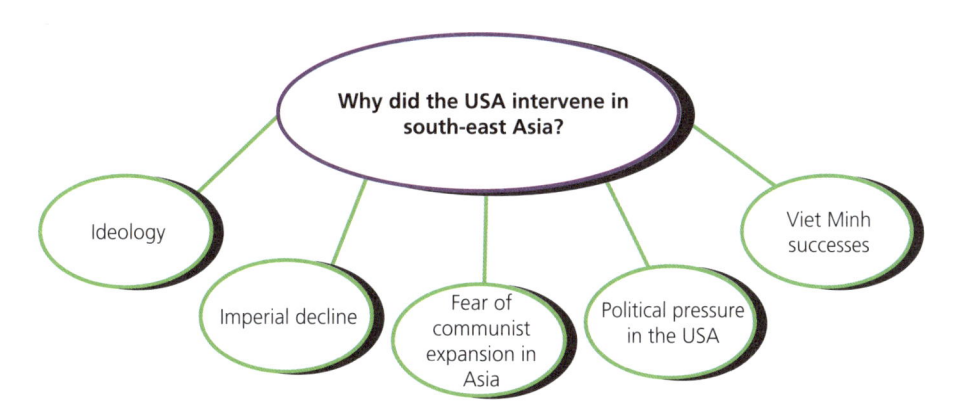

**Why did the USA intervene in south-east Asia?**
- Ideology
- Imperial decline
- Fear of communist expansion in Asia
- Political pressure in the USA
- Viet Minh successes

# Simple essay style

Below is a sample exam-style question. Use your own knowledge and the information on the opposite page to produce a plan for an answer to this question. Choose four general points, and provide three pieces of specific information to support each general point. Once you have planned your essay, write the introduction and conclusion for the essay. The introduction should list the points to be discussed in the essay. The conclusion should summarise the key points and justify which point was the most important.

Why did Truman and Eisenhower support the French in south-east Asia in the period 1950–54?

# Turning assertion into argument

Below are a sample exam-style question and a series of assertions. Read the exam-style question and then add a justification to each of the assertions to turn it into an argument.

Why did Truman and Eisenhower support the French in south-east Asia in the period 1950–54?

*Fear of communist expansion in Asia was one reason why Truman and Eisenhower sent aid to the French because*
_____
_____

*Political pressure in the USA was one reason why Truman sent aid to the French because*
_____
_____

*Viet Minh successes were one reason why Eisenhower sent aid to the French because*
_____
_____

Section 2: The ideological struggle in south-east Asia in the early 1950s

# The foundation of SEATO

Revised

## The US reaction to the Geneva Conference

### Domino Theory

Eisenhower regarded the Geneva Conference as a failure. He recognised that the 1956 election, proposed in the Geneva Accords, would lead to a communist victory. As early as April 1954, Eisenhower had stated his belief that the loss of Vietnam to communism would inspire communist uprisings in adjoining countries. This belief was known as the **Domino Theory**.

### The division of Vietnam

Eisenhower refused to sign the Geneva Accords, but he did pledge to respect the terms of the agreement. However, the Eisenhower administration believed that the division of Vietnam should be permanent. Consequently, the administration began to plan ways in which it could support the creation of an independent and democratic southern Vietnam.

The first step towards a democratic southern Vietnam was French withdrawal. Eisenhower knew that one of the main reasons that the communists were popular was their fight against **colonial rule**. Once the French had withdrawn and southern Vietnam was independent, Eisenhower hoped that communism would lose its appeal. Additionally, the USA could offer aid and advice directly to the new independent government.

The second step towards creating a democratic southern Vietnam was the foundation of a defensive alliance in south-east Asia. This would guarantee the security of southern Vietnam by deterring a communist invasion.

### The foundation of SEATO

In order to prevent the spread of communism in south-east Asia, Eisenhower began negotiations with countries in the **Pacific Rim**. As a result SEATO (South-East Asia Treaty Organisation) was founded. SEATO was established by the South-East Asia Collective Defence Treaty signed in the Philippines in September 1954.

The members of SEATO included Britain and France, who retained colonies in the region. In addition, Japan, the Philippines, Australia, New Zealand, South Korea, Pakistan, and Thailand joined the USA in signing the Treaty.

The Treaty had two purposes:

- SEATO members agreed to co-ordinate collective action against communist aggression
- SEATO members agreed to protect southern Vietnam, Cambodia and Laos from attack.

Notably, southern Vietnam, Cambodia and Laos, although not **signatories** to the Treaty, were defended by the Treaty. These countries could not formally sign the Treaty as the Geneva Accords specifically banned them from alliances with either of the superpowers. However, Eisenhower designed the second part of the Treaty to allow for the defence of southern Vietnam, Cambodia and Laos in a way that did not conflict with the Geneva Accords.

### The foundation of southern Vietnam

Eisenhower's plan for an independent South Vietnam began to take shape in 1955. Ngo Dinh Diem, Prime Minister of the southern region of Vietnam, held a **referendum** to allow the people of southern Vietnam to create their own state and reject reunification. The referendum coincided with French withdrawal from the region. The referendum resulted in the creation of the Republic of Vietnam, which became known as South Vietnam, and Diem became its first president. Diem's victory had US approval as Diem was known to be anti-communist.

## Develop the detail

Below are a sample exam-style question and a paragraph written in answer to this question. The paragraph contains a limited amount of detail. Annotate the paragraph to add additional detail to the answer.

How far do you agree that the 'failure' of the Geneva Accords was the main reason for the establishment of SEATO in 1954?

> One reason for the establishment of SEATO in 1954 was the 'failure' of the Geneva Accords. The US President believed that the Geneva Accords had been a failure because they failed to contain communism. Under the Accords, it had been agreed to divide Vietnam, and to reunite it later. Eisenhower believed that this would lead to a communist victory in Vietnam. The Geneva Accords also agreed that France would leave Vietnam and France had been leading the fight against communism in the area. In this way, the perceived failure of the Geneva Accords led Eisenhower to seek an alternative way of containing communism in south-east Asia. Consequently, he formed SEATO.

## Complex essay style

Below are a sample exam-style question, a list of key points to be made in the essay, and a simple introduction and conclusion for the essay. Read the question, the key points, and the introduction and conclusion. Rewrite the introduction and the conclusion in order to develop an argument.

How far do you agree that the 'failure' of the Geneva Accords was the main reason for the establishment of SEATO in 1954?

### Key points

- The 'failure' of the Geneva Accords
- Domino Theory
- US commitment to containment
- Providing security for French Indochina (Vietnam, Cambodia and Laos)
- Providing security for Diem's regime in southern Vietnam

### Introduction

There were five key reasons why SEATO was established in 1954. These were the 'failure' of the Geneva Accords, the Domino Theory, US commitment to containment, the desire to provide security for French Indochina, and the desire to protect Diem's regime in South Vietnam.

### Conclusion

There were five key reasons why SEATO was established in 1954. The most important reason was the 'failure' of the Geneva Accords. This played a more significant role than all of the other factors.

## Recommended reading

Below is a list of suggested further reading on this topic.

- Steve Phillips, *The Cold War: Conflict in Europe and Asia* (pages 78–80). Heinemann, 2001.
- John W. Young and John Kent, *International Relations Since 1945: A Global History* (pages 247–50). Oxford University Press, 2004.
- Robert J. McMahon, *The Cold War: A Very Short Introduction* (pages 47–48). Oxford University Press, 2003.

## Section 2: The ideological struggle in south-east Asia in the early 1950s

## Exam focus

Below is a sample A-grade essay. Read it and the examiner's comments around it.

Why did the USA become involved in south-east Asia in the period 1950–54?

> The introduction indicates that the essay will discuss four major factors. It begins with a clear answer to the question.

There were four reasons why the USA became involved in south-east Asia in the period 1950–54. These were imperial decline in south-east Asia, the USA's ideological opposition to communism, the successes of the Viet Minh, and the perceived failure of the Geneva Accords of 1954.

> The first sentence of the paragraph contains a clear link to the question, suggesting that the paragraph will be focused on the question.

One reason why the USA became involved in south-east Asia in the period 1950–54 was the decline of European Empires in the region. For example, in British Malaya the British Empire was involved in fighting the Malayan National Liberation Army, a communist and nationalist movement dedicated to overthrowing the British Empire. The British fought back with considerable success, but the French had less success fighting the Viet Minh in Vietnam. In 1945, Ho Chi Minh declared the independence of Vietnam from the French Empire. Ho Chi Minh was a communist and the northern part of Vietnam, which he dominated, became a communist regime. In this way, the decline of empires in south-east Asia was one reason why the USA became involved in the region because the US Presidents Truman and Eisenhower wanted to stop the spread of communism but did not trust the French Empire to be able to achieve this without US help.

Another reason why the USA became involved in south-east Asia in the period 1950–54 was the USA's ideological opposition to communism. For example, Truman was committed to standing up to communism as he believed that a single-party dictatorship and an economy dominated by the state were not compatible with the US values of freedom and democracy. Shortly after the end of the Second World War, Truman outlined his view of communism and advocated 'containment', or the Truman Doctrine. This was the belief that the USA had a moral mission to prevent the spread of communism. In this way, ideological factors help to explain US involvement in south-east Asia because the USA viewed communism as an enemy that it had a duty to stand up to.

A third reason why the USA became involved in south-east Asia in the period 1950–54 was Viet Minh successes. For example, by 1952, the Viet Minh had 250,000 professional soldiers and a militia of 2,000,000. Backed by Chinese weapons, and under the leadership of their General Giap, they won a number of important military victories. The Viet Minh were well known for their guerrilla tactics. This form of unconventional warfare was based on hiding and launching surprise attacks. Additionally, the Viet Minh were also able to launch successful conventional attacks such as the 1954 pitched battle at Dien Bien Phu in which Giap's forces attacked a recently constructed French fortress and defeated the French army of 12,000 soldiers. French failures against the Viet Minh concerned Truman and Eisenhower, and persuaded them to commit US resources to contain communism in south-east Asia.

> This paragraph contains a great deal of accurate detail on Viet Minh strategy and successes and a specific example of their most important success in the period.

The final reason why the USA became involved in south-east Asia was the perceived failure of the Geneva Accords of 1954. The Accords were negotiated between France, China and representatives of local communist movements. The USA hoped that the Geneva Accords would stop the spread of communism in south-east Asia. However, the agreement to hold a nationwide election in Vietnam in 1956 worried Eisenhower because he feared such an election would be won by Ho Chi Minh, leading to a communist government across the whole of Vietnam. In response, Eisenhower established SEATO, which united countries in the Pacific Rim, including Australia, Pakistan and Thailand, in a pact against communism. Additionally, Eisenhower began sending aid directly to the independent government of South Vietnam. In this way, the perceived failure of the Geneva Accords led to US involvement in south-east Asia because Eisenhower felt it was necessary for the USA to act to prevent Vietnam becoming communist.

> This paragraph addresses US policy under President Eisenhower. Consequently, the essay deals with both of the presidents in power in this period, showing range as well as depth.

In conclusion, there were four reasons why the USA became involved in south-east Asia in the period 1950–54. These were imperial decline in south-east Asia; the USA's ideological opposition to communism; the successes of the Viet Minh; and the perceived failure of the Geneva Accords of 1954. They were all equally important as they all contributed to the US fear that communism would spread through south-east Asia, and consequently to US involvement in the region.

> The conclusion summarises the essay. There is an attempt to develop an overall argument in the final sentence, but the argument that all factors were equally important is weak.

**24/30**
This is a well-focused essay which includes a large amount of relevant detail. Every paragraph presents a coherent analysis of the factor it discusses. Nonetheless, this essay cannot enter Level 5 because the introduction and conclusion simply summarise the essay and there is no attempt to develop an overall argument.

### Moving from Level 4 to Level 5

The exam focus at the end of Section 1 (pages 16–17) provided a Level 5 essay. The essay here achieves Level 4. Read both essays, and the examiner's comments provided. Make a list of the additional features required to push a Level 4 essay into Level 5.

# Section 3:
# Growing US participation in Vietnam, 1954–68

## Eisenhower: limited intervention

### Civil war in Vietnam

Following the creation of South Vietnam, a bitter civil war started between the **Viet Cong**, communist sympathisers in the South, and the **Army of the Republic of Vietnam (ARVN)**. The Viet Cong were backed by Ho Chi Minh and the North Vietnamese Army (NVA). The Viet Cong were also active in Laos and Cambodia, and used a network known as the **Ho Chi Minh Trail** to attack South Vietnam. The Viet Cong were known for using **guerrilla** tactics to attack the ARVN.

### Eisenhower's reasons for involvement with Vietnam

US involvement with Vietnam began with President Truman. President Eisenhower, 1953–61, continued US intervention for the following reasons:

- Senior officials within Eisenhower's administration were committed anti-communists. For example, John Foster Dulles, US Secretary of State under Eisenhower, was a Christian and therefore opposed to atheistic communism.
- 'Rolling back' communism had been an important part of Eisenhower's election campaign. In office, he was obliged to fulfil his promises.
- Eisenhower believed that south-east Asia was strategically important in the context of the Cold War. He believed that a communist victory in Vietnam would lead to communist victories throughout south-east Asia, and therefore a shift in the balance of the Cold War.
- Eisenhower was unable to secure the future of Vietnam through the Geneva Accords and therefore attempted to consolidate a non-communist regime through direct intervention.
- Ngo Dinh Diem was well-connected to the Eisenhower administration and urged the President to support the establishment of an independent South Vietnam.

### Eisenhower's policy in Vietnam

#### US intervention

In order to consolidate the South Vietnamese regime, Eisenhower utilised the Military Assistance Advisory Group (MAAG) which had been set up by Truman to co-ordinate aid to Vietnam. MAAG advisors worked with Diem. In total, Eisenhower sent 1500 military and political advisors. MAAG's political advisors recommended a policy of **land reform** and also advised on campaigning techniques as Diem fought for an independent South Vietnam in 1955.

In addition, Eisenhower sent financial aid; by 1961 this totalled $7 billion. Finally, MAAG helped 1 million Vietnamese leave North Vietnam and relocate to the South.

#### The limits of US intervention

Importantly, Eisenhower believed that the USA's role should be purely advisory. Eisenhower rejected **colonialism** and was proud of the USA's opposition to **imperialism**. Consequently, after becoming president in 1955, Diem enjoyed freedom of action.

Eisenhower ruled out direct military intervention in Vietnam. In 1954, Eisenhower had ruled out a US air strike against the Viet Minh during the Dien Bien Phu crisis (see page 22). He continued this policy following the establishment of South Vietnam. Indeed, he rejected Vice-President Nixon's advice that the USA should use nuclear weapons against Ho Chi Minh and North Vietnam.

### The 1956 elections

Ho Chi Minh still believed that Vietnam was be reunited under his leadership following nationwide elections in 1956. Therefore, he assumed that the creation of South Vietnam was only temporary. However, Diem refused to negotiate with Ho Chi Minh and therefore it was impossible to organise the promised elections. Due to the failure of the 1956 elections, the division of Vietnam remained permanent.

## Delete as applicable

Below are a sample exam-style question and a paragraph written in answer to this question. Read the paragraph and decide which of the possible options (in bold) is most appropriate. Delete the least appropriate options and complete the paragraph by justifying your selection.

How successfully did the USA contain communism in south-east Asia during the 1950s?

> Under Eisenhower, the USA was successful in containing communism in south-east Asia to a **great/fair/limited** extent. For example, Eisenhower committed US personnel and money to consolidating the South Vietnamese regime following the Geneva Accords. He made use of the Military Assistance Advisory Group, which had been set up by Truman, in order to help coordinate South Vietnamese defences against the Viet Cong. Equally, he increased the number of advisors to 1500. Finally, he sent political advisors to try and ensure popular support for the South Vietnamese regime. Nonetheless, Eisenhower refused to commit US troops to combat roles and allowed Diem, who was an increasingly unpopular and authoritarian ruler, the freedom to rule South Vietnam in his own way. In this way, under Eisenhower, the USA was successful in containing communism in south-east Asia to a **great/fair/limited** extent because _____
> _____
> _____
> _____

## Simple essay style

Below is a sample exam-style question. Use your own knowledge and the information on the opposite page to produce a plan for an answer to this question. Choose four general points, and provide three pieces of specific information to support each general point. Once you have planned your essay, write the introduction and conclusion for the essay. The introduction should list the points to be discussed in the essay. The conclusion should summarise the key points and justify which point was the most important.

Why did Eisenhower continue US involvement in south-east Asia in the period 1953–61?

**Section 3:** Growing US participation in Vietnam, 1954–68

## The relationship between the USA and Diem

### Diem's supporters

Diem's relationship with the USA was complicated. He had the backing of important US **Congressmen**, including Mike Mansfield and future President John F. Kennedy. Notably, none of Diem's US supporters was an expert in south-east Asia. Therefore, while Diem enjoyed more US support than any other South Vietnamese politician, it did not mean that he was the best qualified candidate to rule South Vietnam.

### Diem and Eisenhower

In June 1954, Diem became Prime Minister of southern Vietnam. He immediately broke with tradition by seeking US help rather than turning to the French. This suited Eisenhower who had doubts about the French regime. He was therefore eager to step in and support Vietnamese politicians who were in favour of independence but not of communism.

Eisenhower was considerably less impressed by Diem than Mansfield and Kennedy. Indeed, Eisenhower viewed Diem as the best of a bad bunch. Nonetheless, Eisenhower believed Diem worth backing. In this way, Diem ensured that US aid continued following the establishment of South Vietnam in 1955.

### Democracy in South Vietnam

Eisenhower was keen to turn South Vietnam into a thriving democracy. However, there were significant concerns in Eisenhower's government about the 1955 referendum on an independent South Vietnam (see page 24). Diem used tactics such as intimidation to win. For example, he poured chilli sauce into the mouths and noses of his opponents' supporters. He also falsified the election results. In Saigon, for example, Diem claimed the support of 600,000 voters although only 450,000 were registered to vote. Indeed, US advisors believed that his claim to have won 98.2 per cent of the vote was wildly exaggerated.

Eisenhower was concerned that the events of 1955 showed that Diem was not fully committed to democracy. Even so, Diem's ability to win the election persuaded Eisenhower that he was a capable politician and therefore deserved US support.

### Diem's visit to the USA

Diem visited the USA in 1957. During the visit, Eisenhower described him as the 'miracle man' of Asia. Eisenhower encouraged him to respect civil rights in South Vietnam and to permit a free press and much greater political freedom for his opponents. However, while Diem was happy to take Eisenhower's praise, he did not take Eisenhower's advice.

### Corruption in South Vietnam

Eisenhower was also concerned about the high levels of corruption in Diem's regime. For example, Diem's family used their connections to enrich themselves. Additionally, Diem appointed his family to senior positions. He even influenced the Catholic Church, which appointed Diem's brother, Ngo Dinh Thuc, as the highest ranking bishop in South Vietnam.

### Catholics and Buddhists

Finally, the Eisenhower administration was concerned about the treatment of Buddhists in South Vietnam. Diem's family were Catholic and favoured the South Vietnamese Catholic minority. By alienating the Buddhist majority, Diem limited his support base. Eisenhower was concerned that without the support of the majority of the people, Diem's regime would be vulnerable to communist opposition.

## Complete the paragraph

Below are a sample exam-style question and a paragraph written in answer to this question. The paragraph contains a point and specific examples, but lacks a concluding explanatory link back to the question. Complete the paragraph adding this link in the space provided.

> How far do you agree that the US provided support to South Vietnam in the period 1954–61 due to pressure from the US Congress?

One reason why the US provided support to South Vietnam in the period 1954–61 was support for Diem from the US Congress.

_____

_____

_____

_____

Congress put pressure on Eisenhower to back Diem's regime and therefore was one reason why the US provided support to South Vietnam in the period 1954 to 1961.

## You're the examiner

Below are a sample exam-style question and a paragraph written in answer to this question. Read the paragraph and the mark scheme provided on page 3. Decide which level you would award the paragraph. Write the level below, along with a justification for your choice.

> How far do you agree that Eisenhower's ideological opposition to communism was the main reason for US involvement in south-east Asia in the period 1953–61?

One reason for US involvement in south-east Asia in the period 1953–61 was the perceived failure of the Geneva Accords. For example, Eisenhower was worried that the commitment in the Geneva Accords of 1954 to hold nationwide elections in Vietnam in 1956 would lead to a communist victory. Worse still, the Geneva Accords proposed reuniting Vietnam, therefore a communist victory in the 1956 elections would lead to the reunification of Vietnam under the communist Ho Chi Minh, a man Eisenhower believed was a 'Soviet puppet'. He was also concerned that a communist victory in Vietnam would lead to the fall of Cambodia and Laos to communism. This view was known as the Domino Theory and meant that Eisenhower believed that the fall of one country to communism would inevitably lead to the fall of the whole region. In this way, the Geneva Accords were one reason for US involvement because their perceived failure led Eisenhower to believe that US involvement was necessary to stop the spread of communism in south-east Asia.

Level: _____  Reason for choosing this level:

_____

_____

Section 3: Growing US participation in Vietnam, 1954–68

## Kennedy: motivation for continuing involvement in Vietnam

On becoming the USA's new Democrat President in 1961, Kennedy inherited a commitment to support Diem's regime. He quickly increased the level of US support.

### Why did Kennedy increase commitment to Vietnam?

#### Political reasons

The Cold War was a big issue in the 1960 Presidential election campaign and Kennedy publicly committed himself to standing up to communism. Following Truman's 'loss' of China, the **Democratic Party** had a reputation for being 'soft on communism'. Kennedy felt compelled to counter this.

Kennedy's first attempt to stand up to communism in Cuba had been a fiasco. Kennedy had supported a **CIA** initiative to overthrow the communist government in Cuba. The CIA-backed invasion of the Bay of Pigs, which took place in April 1961, was a failure and made Kennedy's Cold War strategy vulnerable to criticism. Kennedy hoped to restore his reputation as a 'cold warrior' by standing up to communism in Vietnam.

The French President, Charles de Gaulle, argued that the USA was forced to back the South Vietnamese government due to the fact that no US President wanted to be blamed for losing Vietnam to communism. This criticism was known as the **Quagmire Theory** or the **Commitment Trap**.

#### Personal conviction

- Kennedy refused to 'appease' communism. He did not want a repeat of Britain's appeasement of fascism in the 1930s. In 1940, Kennedy had completed his thesis, 'Appeasement in Munich', arguing that the USA had a moral duty to stand up to dictatorship and defend freedom.
- Kennedy, like Eisenhower before him, believed in the **Domino Theory**.
- Kennedy had a personal relationship with Diem, which was strengthened by the fact that they shared the same Catholic faith.
- Kennedy believed that, as a communist, Ho Chi Minh was bound to work with either Russia or China. Therefore, he viewed him as an enemy in the context of the Cold War and did not explore the possibility of negotiating with him.

#### Senior advisors

- Robert McNamara, the US Defence Secretary, was extremely influential within the Kennedy government. McNamara favoured military solutions to the problems of South Vietnam. McNamara was convinced that the USA could defeat communism in Vietnam due to the superiority of the US military.
- Dean Rusk, US Secretary of State, shared Kennedy's view that the USA should not appease communist aggression. Consequently, he supported McNamara's analysis of the situation in Vietnam and supported continuing and deepening US involvement.

#### Laos

- Kennedy believed that Laos was in a similar position to Vietnam: during 1960, it appeared that communists, backed by Russia, would seize power in Laos. In 1961, Kennedy sent advisors to work with the non-communist government.
- The policy led to the formation of a coalition government, which prevented communists seizing control.
- Kennedy felt his policy had successfully neutralised the threat of communism in Laos. He believed that the same approach would work in Vietnam.

## Spot the mistake

Below are a sample exam-style question and a paragraph written in answer to this question. Why does this paragraph not get into Level 4? Once you have identified the mistake, rewrite the paragraph so that it displays the qualities of Level 4. The mark scheme on page 3 will help you.

Why did the USA become increasingly involved in south-east Asia in the period 1954–63?

> One reason why Kennedy became involved in south-east Asia was because of his ideological and religious beliefs. Kennedy had been critical of the policy of appeasement in Europe during the 1930s and did not want the USA to make the same mistake that Britain had made when it failed to stand up to fascism. Kennedy also believed in the Domino Theory, the idea that once one nation in south-east Asia fell to communism, the rest of the region would inevitably follow. Equally, as a Catholic, Kennedy believed that the USA had a moral duty to fight for freedom. Finally, Kennedy had a friendship with Diem, the South Vietnamese President, a relationship that was strengthened by their shared Catholic faith. In this way, Kennedy became involved in south-east Asia because of his personal conviction that the USA must stand up to communism.

## Eliminate irrelevance

Below are a sample exam-style question and a paragraph written in answer to this question. Read the paragraph and identify parts of the paragraph that are not directly relevant to the question. Draw a line through the information that is irrelevant and justify your deletions in the margin.

How far do you agree that Kennedy's main motivation for continuing US involvement in south-east Asia was to counter accusations that the Democratic Party was 'soft on communism'?

> One reason why Kennedy continued US involvement in south-east Asia was his desire to counter accusations that the Democratic Party was 'soft on communism'. In 1949, Truman was accused of 'losing China' to communism due to his 'failure' to stop Mao Zedong's revolution. Mao was a communist who later launched the Great Leap Forward. Following the Chinese Revolution, the Republican Party accused the Democratic Party of being 'soft on communism'. In addition, Kennedy's most high-profile attempt to stand up to communism had been a failure. In April 1961, Kennedy authorised a CIA-backed invasion of communist Cuba. CIA stands for the Counter-Intelligence Agency and is the US government organisation that has the job of protecting the USA from foreign threats. The 1961 'Bay of Pigs Incident' was a disaster, and allowed the Republicans to criticise Kennedy's Cold War strategy. France was also seen as being unable to stand up to communism because they were never able to defeat Ho Chi Minh. In this way, Kennedy continued US involvement in south-east Asia in order to avoid further accusations that, as a Democrat, he was 'soft on communism'.

Section 3: Growing US participation in Vietnam, 1954–68

# Kennedy: deepening involvement in Vietnam

Revised

## Kennedy's policy towards Vietnam

Kennedy's plan for providing support to Diem was set out in National Security Action Memorandum 52 (NSAM 52). In addition, Kennedy sent political and economic advisors to consolidate Diem's regime.

> ### National Security Action Memorandum 52 (NSAM 52), May 1961
>
> NSAM 52 committed the USA to counter the communist threat and accelerate US involvement in Vietnam in the following ways:
> - Political involvement: sending political advisors
> - Economic involvement: providing financial support
> - Military involvement: providing advice and hardware

In practice, NSAM 52 resulted in the following military aid, and political and economic advice:

| Military aid | Political and economic advisors |
| --- | --- |
| • Kennedy formed the Military Assistance Command, Vietnam (MACV) to co-ordinate military aid. It replaced MAAG, which had been created by Truman.<br>• Kennedy increased the number of military advisors:<br>  – 1960: 800<br>  – 1961: 2000<br>  – 1962: 12,000<br>  – 1963: 16,000.<br>• Kennedy increased the military training budget:<br>  – 1960: $220 million<br>  – 1961: $262 million.<br>• Kennedy sent **Special Forces** to train the ARVN.<br>• Kennedy initiated Operation Ranch Hand in 1962, spraying thousands of acres of forests with **defoliants** and pesticides in order to remove the Viet Cong's cover and destroy their food supplies.<br>• Kennedy authorised the deployment of US troops to perform **reconnaissance** missions to assist the ARVN.<br>• Kennedy authorised the deployment of US helicopters to support ARVN troops. | • In 1962 US advisors recommended the creation of **strategic hamlets** to protect and isolate southern peasants from the Viet Cong. By mid-1963, 7000 strategic hamlets had been created.<br>• Kennedy appointed a new US ambassador, Henry Cabot Lodge, to South Vietnam in order to co-ordinate American aid.<br>• Lodge recommended that Diem's regime should allow greater political and religious freedom to South Vietnamese citizens.<br>• Economic advisors recommended a greater redistribution of wealth to create greater economic equality. They hoped that this would weaken the appeal of communism. |

## How successful was Kennedy's strategy?

### Military aid

US military aid was unable to stop an escalation in the civil war. Moreover, it was not effective in combating the Viet Cong. The Battle of Ap Bac (January 1963) demonstrated the failings of Kennedy's strategy as ARVN troops, equipped with US weapons and outnumbering the Viet Cong four to one, were still unable to win a military victory.

### Political and economic advice

Equally, US advice was sometimes ineffective and sometimes ignored. The strategic hamlets failed to stop the Viet Cong because they were easily infiltrated by Viet Cong agents. In addition, Diem was unwilling to allow a redistribution of wealth. Furthermore, Lodge's advice to permit greater religious tolerance was ignored and in 1963 Diem outlawed the use of Buddhist flags. Famously, Buddhist monk Thich Quang Duc protested against Diem's ban by **self-immolating**.

## The coup against Diem, 1963

Lodge was complicit in the assassination of Diem. Senior figures in the ARVN plotted to overthrow Diem due to the corruption and unpopularity of his regime. Lodge was consulted and did nothing to stop the coup. At the beginning of November 1963, Diem was murdered, and his government was overthrown. Kennedy was horrified.

## Spectrum of significance

Below are a sample exam-style question and a list of general points which could be used to answer the question. Use your own knowledge and the information on the opposite page to reach a judgement about the importance of these general points to the question posed. Write numbers on the spectrum below to indicate their relative importance. Having done this, write a brief justification of your placement, explaining why some of these factors are more important than others. The resulting diagram could form the basis of an essay plan.

How successful was Kennedy's intervention in south-east Asia?

1. Political involvement
2. Economic involvement
3. Military involvement

⬅——————————————————➡

Very important                             Less important

## RAG – Rate the timeline

Below are a sample exam-style question and a timeline. Read the question, study the timeline and, using three coloured pens, put a red, amber or green star next to the events to show:

- red – events and policies that have no relevance to the question
- amber – events and policies that have some significance to the question
- green – events and policies that are directly relevant to the question.

1. Why did the USA become increasingly involved in south-east Asia in the period 1954–63?

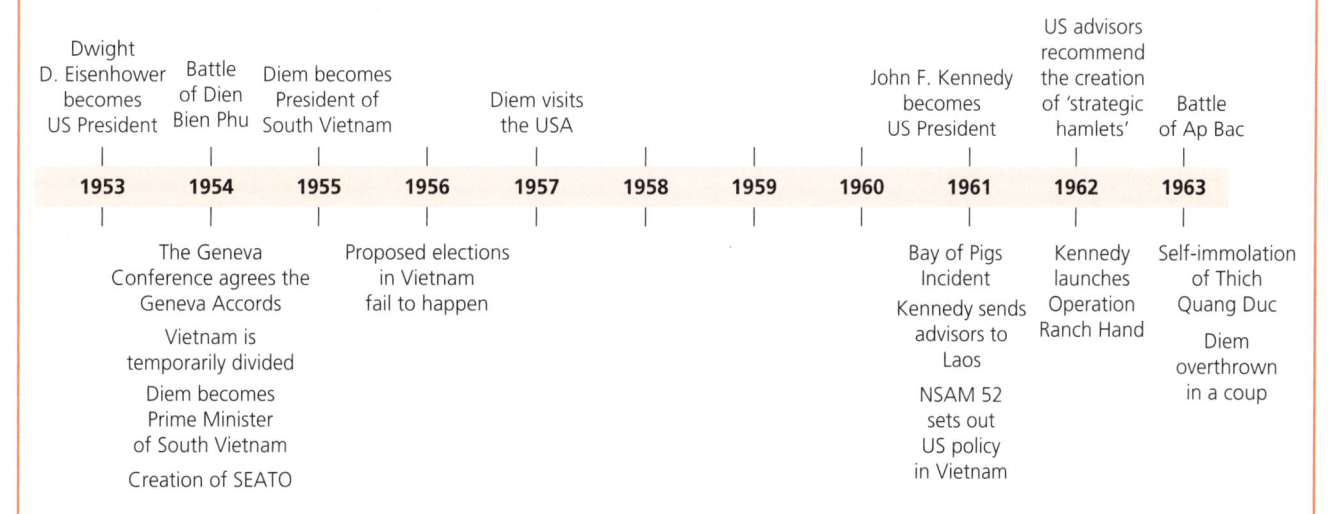

**Timeline (1953–1963):**

Above the line:
- 1953: Dwight D. Eisenhower becomes US President
- 1954: Battle of Dien Bien Phu
- 1955: Diem becomes President of South Vietnam
- 1957: Diem visits the USA
- 1961: John F. Kennedy becomes US President
- 1962: US advisors recommend the creation of 'strategic hamlets'
- 1963: Battle of Ap Bac

Below the line:
- 1954: The Geneva Conference agrees the Geneva Accords; Vietnam is temporarily divided; Diem becomes Prime Minister of South Vietnam; Creation of SEATO
- 1956: Proposed elections in Vietnam fail to happen
- 1961: Bay of Pigs Incident; Kennedy sends advisors to Laos; NSAM 52 sets out US policy in Vietnam
- 1962: Kennedy launches Operation Ranch Hand
- 1963: Self-immolation of Thich Quang Duc; Diem overthrown in a coup

Now repeat the activity with the following questions. You could use different colours, or number your stars 1, 2 or 3.

2. How successful was US policy in south-east Asia in the period 1954–63?
3. How far do you agree that Eisenhower and Kennedy were equally responsible for deepening US involvement in south-east Asia in the period 1954–63?

# Section 3: Growing US participation in Vietnam, 1954–68

## Johnson: initial escalation

Following Kennedy's assassination in November 1963, Lyndon B. Johnson, the US Vice-President, took office as President. Initially, he continued Kennedy's approach to Vietnam. However, in August 1964, US policy took a new direction as Johnson despatched US troops to support the ARVN in the civil war.

### Johnson and Vietnam

Johnson continued US involvement for the following reasons:

- Following Diem's assassination, the government of South Vietnam was extremely unstable and unable to co-ordinate effective resistance to the Viet Cong.
- By mid-1964, over a third of South Vietnam was in Viet Cong hands, and Johnson became convinced that the Viet Cong was winning the civil war.
- Johnson did not want to 'lose Vietnam' as he was facing a Presidential election in November 1964.
- McNamara continued as Defence Secretary and advised Johnson to continue to support South Vietnam.

### Escalation

#### Covert operations

Johnson's initial response to the increasing difficulties of the South Vietnamese government was to send more money and more advisors. He also authorised US Special Forces to engage in **covert operations**. In this sense, he authorised direct military intervention but without alerting the public or requiring the approval of **Congress**. Johnson was concerned that publically deploying US troops in South Vietnam would be unpopular and would jeopardise his chances of winning the 1964 Presidential election.

### The Gulf of Tonkin Incident (August 1964)

The ARVN launched raids on North Vietnamese coastal towns, supported by US ships stationed in the Gulf of Tonkin (see map on page 22). Their intention was to weaken the communist regime in the North and disrupt northern supplies reaching the Viet Cong. The NVA retaliated and opened fire on the USS *Maddox*, a US ship stationed in the region.

The Gulf of Tonkin Incident, as it became known, outraged the US public and persuaded Congress to pass the Gulf of Tonkin Resolution.

> **The Gulf of Tonkin Resolution**
>
> Technically, the Gulf of Tonkin Resolution did not authorise war between the USA and the Viet Cong. Rather, it gave Johnson the authority to 'use all means necessary' to defend US personnel in the region. Nonetheless, Johnson used the Resolution to despatch US troops to fight the Viet Cong.

### Operation Rolling Thunder (February 1965)

Johnson's first big initiative was Operation Rolling Thunder, a systematic campaign of bombing raids designed to disrupt supplies to the Viet Cong and demoralise the population of North Vietnam. Targets included Hanoi, the Northern capital. The bombing campaign continued until 1968. It made use of US B-52 bombers, each of which could carry 30 tonnes of bombs, capable of levelling 1.5 square miles. Operation Rolling Thunder failed to have a significant impact on Viet Cong supplies because it did not target the Viet Cong's major supply route, the Ho Chi Minh Trail, which ran through Cambodia and Laos. Furthermore, it did not have the desired effect the morale of the North Vietnamese as the bombing raids turned the North Vietnamese against the Americans rather than against their own government.

### US ground troops

Johnson also authorised the deployment of ground troops to defend US **installations** in South Vietnam. The first troops arrived in March 1965 and were tasked with protecting the Da Nang air force base. By July, there were 125,000 US soldiers in South Vietnam.

### Simple essay style

Below is a sample exam-style question. Use your own knowledge and the information on the opposite page to produce a plan for an answer to this question. Choose four general points, and provide three pieces of specific information to support each general point. Once you have planned your essay, write the introduction and conclusion for the essay. The introduction should list the points to be discussed in the essay. The conclusion should summarise the key points and justify which point was the most important.

Why did President Johnson escalate US involvement in the Vietnam War in 1964?

### Turning assertion into argument

Below are a sample exam-style question and a series of assertions. Read the exam-style question and then add a justification to each of the assertions to turn it into an argument.

How far do you agree that the Gulf of Tonkin Incident was the main reason for the escalation of US involvement in south-east Asia in the years 1954–65?

*The Gulf of Tonkin Incident was the main reason for the escalation of US involvement in south-east Asia in the years 1954–65 in the sense that*

*The Geneva Accords were another reason for the escalation of US involvement in south-east Asia in the years 1954–65 in the sense that*

*Johnson's desire not to 'lose Vietnam' was another reason for the escalation of US involvement in south-east Asia in the years 1954–65 in the sense that*

# Section 3: Growing US participation in Vietnam, 1954–68

## The nature of the Vietnam War

### Guerrilla warfare

Johnson and his advisors believed that the Vietnam War was a **war of attrition** in which the largest army would win. They prepared for a traditional war based on **pitched battles**. However, the Viet Cong quickly adopted **guerrilla** tactics.

#### Guerrilla tactics

The Viet Cong divided their forces into small units. They would only fight small groups of US soldiers, and then only at close range. These guerrilla tactics undercut the USA's superiority in terms of numbers and weapons.

Guerrilla tactics included:

- 'hit and run' raids
- sabotage of US equipment
- hidden traps such as tripwires and covered pits
- stealth tactics: hiding in the jungle or amongst the general population.

### The US Army and guerrilla tactics

The US Army was not trained to counter guerrilla tactics. In response to guerrilla attacks, the USA extended Operation Ranch Hand (see page 34), using **Napalm** and **Agent Orange** to destroy the Viet Cong's jungle cover. In addition, US forces were involved in 'clear and hold' operations and the Phoenix Program.

#### Napalm

Napalm is a highly flammable and sticky chemical jelly. The USA used it to destroy areas of jungle in which the Viet Cong were hiding. The use of Napalm often resulted in the deaths of civilians.

#### Agent Orange

Agent Orange is a toxic chemical used to kill trees. The US air force undertook 6542 'spraying missions', covering more than 10 per cent of Vietnam. Their aim was to destroy the jungle cover of their enemies. Agent Orange had a considerable impact on the civilian population, leading to an estimated 400,000 casualties.

### 'Clear and hold'

'Clear and hold' operations involved US troops patrolling villages in South Vietnam in order to root out communist infiltration. By the end of 1969, the South Vietnamese government had re-established control of over 50 per cent of rural South Vietnam.

### The Phoenix Program

The Phoenix Program, launched in 1967, required US troops to identify and capture Viet Cong personnel. In many cases, captured Viet Cong were tortured. By 1972, 20,000 Viet Cong officers had been executed.

### Morale and discipline amongst US troops

US troops were poorly trained for jungle warfare. The average age of the US troops was nineteen, and most had been conscripted and therefore had not chosen to sign up and fight the war. Moreover, the Viet Cong's tactics meant that the soldiers were always vulnerable to attack. Notably, US soldiers were at their safest during pitched battles, the type of warfare they had prepared for. Lack of relevant training, continual fear of attack, and the pointlessness of daily operations led to a decline in morale and discipline.

The US Army attempted to counter this by providing luxuries for their troops. These included recreational activities such as baseball and swimming, and food such as ice cream and burgers. Troops were also sent on rest and recuperation (R&R) breaks to Thailand and Japan.

Some historians claim that, rather than improving morale, the luxuries provided by the army made the soldiers 'soft'. Morale was also sapped by declining support for the war from home. As a result discipline declined further, leading to drug abuse and **fragging**.

## Mind Map

Use the information in Section 3 so far to add detail to the mind map below.

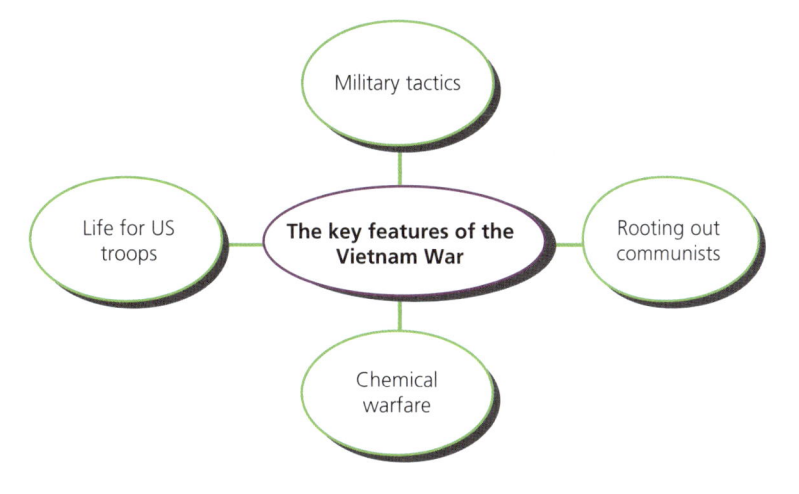

- The key features of the Vietnam War
  - Military tactics
  - Rooting out communists
  - Chemical warfare
  - Life for US troops

## Complex essay style

Below are a sample exam-style question, a list of key points to be made in the essay, and a simple introduction and conclusion for the essay. Read the question, the key points, and the introduction and conclusion. Rewrite the introduction and the conclusion in order to develop an argument.

How far did US policy in Vietnam change in the period 1954–64?

### Key points

- CHANGE – Kennedy sent Special Forces to support the ARVN
- CHANGE – Congress passed the Gulf of Tonkin Resolution
- CHANGE – Johnson committed combat troops
- CONTINUITY – containment remained a priority
- CONTINUITY – each successive president escalated involvement in Vietnam

### Introduction

> There was clearly evidence of change and continuity in US policy in Vietnam in the period 1954–64. Policy changed in that Kennedy sent Special Forces to support the ARVN, Congress passed the Gulf of Tonkin Resolution, and Johnson committed combat troops to fight the war. However, policy remained the same in that containment remained a priority, and each successive president escalated involvement in Vietnam.

### Conclusion

> In conclusion, there was clearly evidence of change and continuity in US policy in Vietnam in the period 1954–64.

Section 3: Growing US participation in Vietnam, 1954–68

## Johnson: massive escalation

Revised

### Johnson's war, 1965–67

The initial deployment of US ground troops in South Vietnam was primarily defensive: they were tasked with protecting US bases in South Vietnam. However, during 1965, General **William Westmoreland** committed US troops to 'search and destroy' missions. Troop numbers increased steadily from 1965 to 1968.

| Year | Total number of US troops in Vietnam |
|---|---|
| 1965 | 184,300 |
| 1966 | 385,300 |
| 1967 | 485,600 |
| 1968 | 536,100 |

### The Battle of Chu Lai (August 1965)

In July 1965, Johnson approved the deployment of a further 50,000 US troops to South Vietnam. The Battle of Chu Lai was the first significant US success. Westmoreland said that the pitched battle was a victory for the USA because US soldiers had killed 600 Viet Cong and only lost 50 of their own men. Johnson and his advisors took the 'kill ratio' as a sign that the war in Vietnam was winnable and could be dealt with quickly.

### Search and destroy

Following Chu Lai, the Viet Cong adopted guerrilla tactics. In response General Westmoreland used ground troops to conduct 'search and destroy' missions. These focused on routing out Viet Cong supporters in South Vietnamese territory and, on occasion, destroying whole villages that supported the Viet Cong. However, only 1 per cent of search and destroy missions successfully engaged the enemy.

### Extending aerial bombardment

During 1966, the USA extended its bombing raids. In June 1966, the air force began to target oil depots around Hanoi, the capital of North Vietnam. By July, US planes had established their dominance over the whole of North Vietnamese air space and were flying as far north as the Chinese border.

### 'Hearts and minds'

Johnson realised that, in order to win the military battle, he needed to win the 'hearts and minds' – the loyalty and trust – of the South Vietnamese people. The Vietnam War was a civil war, and the only justification for the presence of US troops was to support the South Vietnamese. However, US military action undermined support for the USA. For example, search and destroy campaigns and the use of Napalm and defoliants resulted in the destruction of 3 million homes in South Vietnam by the end of 1966. By 1968, the USA had made 4 million South Vietnamese people homeless. Consequently, US military action alienated the people of South Vietnam, making them more willing to support the Viet Cong.

### US success and failure by 1967

| Success | Failure |
|---|---|
| • General Westmoreland consistently reported that the 'kill ratio' favoured the USA. In most engagements the USA lost one tenth of the men lost by their opponents. | • In spite of these high 'kill rates' the USA's enemies found it very easy to replenish their armies. By 1967, communist forces operating in South Vietnam included:<br>– 50,000 NVA troops<br>– 225,000 Viet Cong<br>– 150,000 local **militias**.<br>• Bombing failed to disrupt the Viet Cong's supply chain as much of the Ho Chi Minh Trail was outside Vietnam and not subject to US bombing.<br>• The US Army were not prepared for guerrilla tactics.<br>• The 1967 South Vietnamese election showed that only 35 per cent of South Vietnamese people were prepared to back the American-sponsored government. |

## Identify an argument

Below are a series of definitions, a sample exam-style question and two sample conclusions. One of the conclusions achieves a high level because it contains an argument. The other achieves a lower level because it contains only description and assertion. Identify which is which. The mark scheme on page 3 will help you.

- Description: a detailed account.
- Assertion: a statement of fact or an opinion which is not supported by a reason.
- Reason: a statement which explains or justifies something.
- Argument: an assertion justified with a reason.

How successful was Johnson's policy in Vietnam between August 1964 and December 1967?

### Sample 1

In conclusion, Johnson's policy in Vietnam was a partial success. In military terms, General Westmoreland was able to claim success in terms of the 'kill ratio'. However, Westmoreland's analysis was flawed due to the scale of communist forces. In terms of 'hearts and minds', Johnson's policy was undoubtedly a failure due to the fact that US policy was counter-productive as it destroyed the homes of the people it was designed to protect. Consequently, Johnson's policy was a partial success in military terms, but a disaster in terms of winning over the population of South Vietnam.

### Sample 2

In conclusion, Johnson's policy in Vietnam was both a success and a failure. The USA was successful because a higher number of communists were being killed than US soldiers. However, the USA failed because it did not win the support of the South Vietnamese people due to policies which destroyed their homes.

## You're the examiner

Below are a sample exam-style question and a paragraph written in answer to this question. Read the paragraph and the mark scheme provided on page 3. Decide which level you would award the paragraph. Write the level below, along with a justification for your choice.

How successful was Johnson's policy in Vietnam between August 1964 and December 1967?

Johnson became president in 1963, following the death of President Kennedy. After becoming president, he passed a resolution about Vietnam which led to the use of Napalm and Operation Ranch Hand. Kennedy had also done things in Vietnam, because he did not want to be seen to lose Vietnam like Truman lost China. However, Kennedy did not do as much as Johnson. The resolution allowed Johnson to do much more than Kennedy had done. Johnson was also worried about losing Vietnam and wanted to be successful in not losing it.

Level:      Reason for choosing this level:

_____

_____

## The significance of the Tet Offensive

### A turning point in the war

The biggest turning point in the war occurred in 1968. Communist forces prepared a trap for Westmoreland's forces, and in the middle of a temporary ceasefire, unleashed the Tet Offensive across South Vietnam. The Offensive was a military failure but a propaganda success for the communist forces. Significantly, the Offensive forced Johnson to rethink his strategy.

### Giap's trap

In late 1967, Giap began to build up NVA forces at Khe Sanh, north of the **Demilitarised Zone**. Westmoreland was convinced that the NVA were preparing for a major pitched battle against US forces. He sent 50,000 US troops to the DMZ in preparation. On 20 January, Giap's forces attacked the USA as expected. However, the Khe Sanh Offensive was a diversion designed to distract US forces from the forthcoming Tet Offensive.

### The Tet Offensive

On 30 January (Vietnamese New Year in 1968), NVA forces and the Viet Cong launched a new offensive from the Ho Chi Minh Trail. The action, known as the Tet Offensive, targeted major cities across the South. The Tet Offensive was a surprise attack as a ceasefire had been agreed for the period of the New Year. It was a big embarrassment for the US Embassy due to the fact that the NVA was able to surround the US Embassy in Saigon. The Offensive was finally suppressed on 24 February.

Westmoreland claimed that the USA had won an important victory pointing to the 10:1 'kill ratio'. Indeed, the Viet Cong were severely weakened. As a result the next offensives, 'mini-Tet' in May and 'Tet III' in August, failed to have a significant impact on the war. Consequently, the NVA played a much greater role following 1968.

### The significance of the Tet Offensive

Despite Westmoreland's claim that the Tet Offensive was a victory for the USA, it was a turning point in terms of US public opinion. The attack had exposed many of the USA's weaknesses:

- US intelligence had failed to predict the Offensive.
- The NVA was able to penetrate territory in South Vietnam as far south as Saigon.
- Johnson's assurances that the USA was winning the war seemed far-fetched.

The Tet Offensive was a psychological shock for the US people. Following the Offensive, an opinion poll showed that two-thirds of the US public believed that no progress had been made since 1965. Respected TV journalist **Walter Cronkite** spoke for the US people when he asked, 'What the hell is going on? I thought we were winning the war.' Following Cronkite's statement, Johnson's approval rating fell from 48 per cent to 36 per cent. Clearly, the Tet Offensive created a public backlash against the Vietnam War.

### Johnson's response

In response to the Tet Offensive, Johnson consulted his '**wise men**', including Dean Acheson and George Ball. They recommended a policy of disengagement and Johnson announced plans for 'de-Americanisation' of the conflict. De-Americanisation meant passing the burden of fighting from US troops to the ARVN. Johnson also announced a de-escalation of the war:

- In March 1968, Johnson publically announced he was seeking peace, and that he would limit bombing raids.
- Peace talks began in Paris in May, but made no progress.
- In October, Johnson ordered a complete halt to the bombing.

## Support or challenge?

Below is a sample exam-style question which asks how far you agree with a specific statement. Below this are a series of general statements which are relevant to the question. Using your own knowledge and the information on the opposite page decide whether these statements support or challenge the statement in the question and tick the appropriate box.

'The Tet Offensive was a failure for the USA.' How far do you agree with this statement?

| Statement | SUPPORT | CHALLENGE |
| --- | --- | --- |
| The Tet Offensive was a military failure for the Viet Cong. | | |
| Viet Cong soldiers surrounded the US Embassy in Saigon. | | |
| The Tet Offensive caught US forces by surprise. | | |
| US troops had a 10:1 kill ratio over Viet Cong troops. | | |
| Mini-Tet and Tet III were failures for the Viet Cong. | | |
| Walter Cronkite spoke out against the war in Vietnam following the Tet Offensive. | | |

## Develop the detail

Below are a sample exam-style question and a paragraph written in answer to this question. The paragraph contains a limited amount of detail. Annotate the paragraph to add additional detail to the answer.

How far do you agree that the Tet Offensive was a turning point in the Vietnam War?

> One way in which the Tet Offensive was a turning point in the Vietnam War was that it exposed the weaknesses in the US strategy in Vietnam. The Tet Offensive showed the US public that enemy forces could reach important sites in South Vietnam. It also showed that US intelligence had misunderstood the situation in Vietnam. Finally, it showed that there was more to winning the Vietnam War than US generals had anticipated. In this way, the Tet Offensive was a turning point in the Vietnam War because it brought the weakness of US military strategy to the attention of the US public, turning many members of the public against the war.

# Section 3: Growing US participation in Vietnam, 1954–68

## Public opinion and the cost of the War

### Opposition to the War

Organised opposition to the war began in 1965, but prior to the Tet Offensive active anti-war feeling never exceeded 10 per cent of the US population.

### Black opposition to the War

There were two major sources of opposition to the War from within the black community. The Civil Rights movement, which had emerged in 1955, was dominated by activists committed to peaceful protest. Their belief in peace and often in pacifism led them to believe that the war in Vietnam was immoral. **Martin Luther King**, the most prominent spokesman for the Civil Rights movement, publically criticised the conduct of the war in 1967.

More radical black campaigners associated with the **Black Power movement** criticised the racial nature of the War. They argued that it was an imperialist war where white US soldiers fought the 'black' Vietnamese.

### Youth culture

The 1960s witnessed the growth of protest movements in the big universities. Student movements were at the forefront of anti-war protest as the majority of soldiers fighting in the war were of university age.

In April 1965, **Students for a Democratic Society (SDS)** organised a 20,000-strong anti-war rally in Washington DC. Bigger marches followed, including a march of 100,000 in Washington in 1967, and a march of 200,000 in New York in the same year.

SDS also organised campus protests such as **teach-ins**. By the end of 1965, 20,000 students had been involved in around 120 teach-ins, the biggest being held in Berkeley, California.

### Opposition to the draft

In order to recruit soldiers for the Vietnam War, Johnson initiated a draft. Once a month, a certain number of men aged between 18 and 25 were 'called up' and required to fight in Vietnam. This draft was unpopular because it was clearly unfair. Wealthy white Americans could avoid the draft by going to university. Working-class and black Americans could not afford to escape by going to university and therefore around 80 per cent of soldiers came from poor or working-class backgrounds. Draft protestors publically objected by burning their **draft cards**.

### The cost of the War

#### The financial cost

Between 1965 and 1973, the US government spent $120 billion on the Vietnam War. Much of this was borrowed. Indeed, in 1965, the US **budget deficit** stood at $1.6 billion, while by 1968 it had reached $25.3 billion.

As a result, Johnson's **Great Society programme**, which was designed to help the USA's poorest citizens, was starved of cash. In fact, the Great Society programme only received $15.5 billion of government spending between 1965 and 1968.

#### The political cost

The War also cost Johnson support in Congress. The Gulf of Tonkin Resolution (August 1964) passed Congress with almost unanimous support. However, by 1967, a number of the President's allies, for example Senator William Fulbright, publically opposed the war. Johnson even lost the support of high-profile 'cold warriors' such as George Kennan, one of the early advocates of containment, and General James M. Gavin, who argued that the War was a waste of money.

> **The 1968 election**
>
> The Vietnam War played a major role in the 1968 Presidential election. Following the Tet Offensive, Johnson withdrew from the presidential race so that he could focus on fighting the war. **Republican** candidate, Richard Nixon, hinted that he had a 'secret plan' to end the Vietnam War. His willingness to withdraw from Vietnam was one of the reasons for his victory in the presidential race.

#### The human cost

| Group | Estimated death toll |
|---|---|
| American soldiers | 58,000 |
| ARVN | 220,000 |
| NVA | 850,000 |
| Viet Cong | 250,000 |
| Civilians | 2,000,000 |

These death tolls include those killed by the use of Agent Orange and Napalm. However, they do not include those wounded or maimed by the War, or the estimated 500,000 children born with birth defects as a result of the use of Agent Orange.

## RAG – Rate the timeline

Below are a sample exam-style question and a timeline. Read the question, study the timeline and, using three coloured pens, put a red, amber or green star next to the events to show:

- red – events and policies that have no relevance to the question
- amber – events and policies that have some significance to the question
- green – events and policies that are directly relevant to the question.

1. How accurate is it to say that the Tet Offensive was the most significant reason for changing public perceptions of the Vietnam War in the period 1964–68?

**Timeline:**

**1964**
- Gulf of Tonkin Incident
- Gulf of Tonkin Resolution
- Johnson initiates 'covert operations' in Vietnam

**1965**
- General Westmoreland commits US troops to 'search and destroy' missions
- SDS organise a 20,000-strong anti-war rally in Washington DC
- Battle of Chu Lai
- Johnson launches Operation Rolling Thunder
- First US ground troops arrive in Vietnam

**1966**
- Escalation of US bombing in Vietnam

**1967**
- South Vietnamese election reveals little support for the US-backed government
- Battle of Khe Sanh
- Martin Luther King speaks out against the Vietnam War
- Johnson launches the Phoenix Program

**1968**
- Tet Offensive
- Mini-Tet
- Paris peace talks begin
- Tet III

Now repeat the activity with the following questions. You could use different colours, or number your stars 1, 2 and 3.

2. How successful was Johnson's policy in Vietnam between 1964 and 1968?
3. Why was the USA unable to defeat communism in south-east Asia in the years 1964–68?

## Complex essay style

Below are a sample exam-style question, a list of key points to be made in the essay, and a simple introduction and conclusion for the essay. Read the question, the key points, and the introduction and conclusion. Rewrite the introduction and the conclusion in order to develop an argument.

How accurate is it to say that by 1968 US involvement in south-east Asia had become too costly to continue?

### Key points

- COST – human cost
- COST – financial cost
- COST – US military failures
- COST – political cost to Johnson
- BENEFIT – US military successes
- BENEFIT – US public support for the war before 1968

### Introduction

*US involvement in south-east Asia was costly in four ways. It was costly in human terms, in financial terms, in terms of US military failure, and it was of political cost to Johnson. However, US involvement in south-east Asia brought benefits in terms of US military successes and continued public support for the war until 1968.*

### Conclusion

*In conclusion, US involvement in south-east Asia was both costly and of benefit to the USA.*

## Recommended reading

Below is a list of suggested further reading on this topic.

- Mike Sewell Clements, *The Cold War*, fourth edition (pages 68–70). Cambridge University Press, 2002.
- Vivienne Sanders, *The USA in Asia* (pages 134–59). Hodder Education, 2010.
- Robert J. McMahon, *The Cold War: A Very Short Introduction* (pages 102–105). Oxford University Press, 1999.

# Section 3: Growing US participation in Vietnam, 1954–68

## Exam focus

Below is a sample A-grade essay. Read it and the examiner's comments around it.

How successful was US policy in Vietnam in the period 1954–68?

*The introduction clearly defines what US policy was designed to achieve in Vietnam and therefore establishes a criteria for success or failure.*

*The introduction indicates that the essay will consider success and failure in terms of different aspects of US policy.*

US policy in Vietnam in the period 1954–68 was designed to contain communism. To this end, the USA sent political and military advisors, and later, ground troops to Vietnam. US policy in Vietnam in the period was largely unsuccessful in terms of providing political and economic advice to the South Vietnamese regime and in terms of winning over the hearts and minds of the Vietnamese people. However, in terms of the kill ratio, the USA was able to claim considerable military success. Nonetheless, the Tet Offensive demonstrated that there was much more to success than winning a military victory.

*By beginning in 1954, the essay clearly addresses the early part of the chronology specified by the question.*

Under Eisenhower, there were some political successes. For example, following the Geneva Accords of 1954, Eisenhower supported the creation of an independent South Vietnam, with Diem as its president from 1955. Diem's regime lasted eight years and was relatively stable. The creation of the South Vietnamese regime stopped the 1956 Vietnam elections which Eisenhower feared would lead to the creation of a communist government under Ho Chi Minh. Nonetheless, Eisenhower's policy did not succeed in creating a democracy in South Vietnam. Diem's regime was highly corrupt. For example, Diem appointed his brothers to senior positions, including that of highest ranking bishop in South Vietnam. In addition, Eisenhower was unable to persuade Diem to stop the persecution of Buddhists in Vietnam. In this way, Eisenhower was only partially successful in preventing the spread of communism to South Vietnam because although Diem's regime was stable it was not popular enough to undermine the appeal of communism in South Vietnam.

*This paragraph opens by comparing the level of success achieved by Kennedy with that of Eisenhower. This helps to build a sustained argument about the level of success throughout the period.*

Kennedy's political and economic aid to Vietnam was less successful. Kennedy sent political and economic advisors as well as a new US ambassador, Henry Cabot Lodge, to South Vietnam. Kennedy recommended greater economic equality in South Vietnam, as well as greater respect for religious freedom. These policies failed as Diem refused to modify his economic or religious policies. Indeed, the Buddhist monk, Thich Quang Duc, famously set himself on fire to protest against Diem's religious intolerance. The final failure of Kennedy's administration was that it allowed the overthrow of Diem himself in a coup in November 1963. Kennedy's policy failed to contain communism in South Vietnam because it failed to stop the fall of South Vietnam's anti-communist government.

The USA's military policy in Vietnam was more successful. Kennedy continued Eisenhower's policy of military advisors, military aid, and the use of defoliants to tackle the Viet Cong. Kennedy increased the number of military advisors from 800 in 1960 to 16,000 in 1963. However, this was not enough to stop the Viet Cong's victory in the Battle of Ap Bac (January 1963). Following the Gulf of Tonkin Incident of August 1964, Johnson committed ground troops. This led to a major US success at the Battle of Chu Lai at which 600 Viet Cong were killed in comparison to only 50 US soldiers. General Westmoreland argued that this kill ratio proved US superiority in the War. In this way, the USA was partially successful in containing communism in the sense that it was able to win significant military victories which limited the spread of communism throughout South Vietnam.

However, Johnson was less successful at winning the hearts and minds of the Vietnamese people. The use of Napalm and Agent Orange led to around 400,000 civilian casualties and 'search and destroy' missions made 4 million South Vietnamese people homeless. In this way, the US military failed to prevent the spread of communist ideas because its own actions alienated the people of South Vietnam, making them more willing to support the Viet Cong.

*This is the second paragraph dealing with Johnson. It effectively contrasts Johnson's 'hearts and minds' policy with his military policy mentioned in the previous paragraph.*

The Tet Offensive of 1968 was a military success for the USA, but a public relations disaster. The Offensive was beaten back by US troops and Westmoreland pointed to the favourable 10:1 kill ratio achieved by US troops. Following the Tet Offensive, the USA had weakened the Viet Cong so much that Mini-Tet and Tet III were failures for the Viet Cong. However, the Tet Offensive embarrassed the USA because it was a clear sign that US intelligence had failed and because the NVA were able to surround the US embassy in Saigon. The Tet Offensive lost the hearts and minds of the US public. Johnson's approval rating fell from 48 per cent to 36 per cent following the Offensive and Walter Cronkite reflected the public mood when he stated 'I thought we were winning the war'. The loss of US support was significant because it put pressure on the US government to end the war. In this way, the Tet Offensive was a failure for the USA because it weakened the government's resolve to continue the fight to contain communism in south-east Asia.

In conclusion, US policy in Vietnam in the period 1954–68 failed in its primary goal of containing communism. In spite of some important military victories, the USA consistently failed to win over the hearts and minds of the South Vietnamese people.

*The conclusion summarises the argument but does not deal with all of the factors discussed in the essay.*

**28/30**
This essay is awarded a mark in the middle of Level 5 as it contains a sustained argument and a good range and depth of accurate and relevant supporting information. However, it does not achieve full marks as the conclusion is weaker than the rest of the essay. The conclusion does not deal with all of the factors discussed in the essay and therefore does not fully analyse US policy across the whole of the period 1954–68.

### Key terms

One of the reasons that this essay achieves so highly is that it clearly states what US policy was designed to achieve in Vietnam and therefore establishes a criteria for success or failure. Another example of an essay question requiring an assessment of the extent of success is below. Draw a plan for your answer to this question. Include a definition of success in your introduction and refer back to this definition in subsequent paragraphs.

> How successful was US intervention in Korea in the period 1950–53?

# Section 4:
# The Nixon presidency and the withdrawal of US forces, 1969–73

## Nixon and Vietnamisation

### 'Peace with honour'

Nixon's aim in Vietnam was to achieve 'peace with honour'. By this, Nixon meant a peace settlement that was not damaging to the interests of the USA.

### Nixon's policy options

Nixon considered three alternative approaches to achieving 'peace with honour'. However, each option had drawbacks.

| Policy option | Drawbacks |
|---|---|
| Complete withdrawal | This would mean betraying South Vietnam, a US ally. In addition, it would make the USA look vulnerable during the Cold War. In this sense, it would achieve peace but without honour. |
| Invade North Vietnam with the aim of ending the war by ending the communist regime. | This risked bringing China into the war, as North Vietnam bordered China. Nixon feared a repeat of the stalemate that had taken place in the Korean War. This option looked likely to prolong the war rather than achieve peace. |
| Using nuclear weapons against North Vietnam | Nixon believed that the US public would not support this option and that China might retaliate. This option also would lead to an escalation of the war, rather than peace. |

### Vietnamisation

None of the new options considered by Nixon would achieve 'peace with honour'. Therefore, Nixon continued Johnson's policy of de-Americanisation in 1969, with a new emphasis on the withdrawal of US troops. Nixon's policy became known as Vietnamisation. The policy put the burden of fighting on ARVN troops. US soldiers played only a supporting role, providing technical support and air power.

Nixon hoped that this would achieve 'peace with honour':

- The phased withdrawal of US troops would diminish opposition to the war in the USA and therefore strengthen Nixon's negotiating position.
- The increased use of ARVN troops would reduce the financial and human cost of the war to the USA. This would also diminish opposition to the war in the USA.
- A combination of well-trained ARVN ground troops and US airpower could maintain pressure on the NVA, forcing North Vietnam to negotiate an end to the war.

### The Guam Doctrine

Nixon's Guam Doctrine provided the public justification for Vietnamisation. In essence, Nixon remained committed to fighting communism. He pledged to provide US military and economic support for the fight against communism, but argued that it was not the USA's responsibility to provide troops. Rather, he argued, local governments should be responsible for providing the manpower needed to fight communism.

### 'Madman Theory'

Although Nixon had privately ruled out the use of nuclear weapons in Vietnam, he never revealed this in public. This was a deliberate strategy known as 'Madman Theory'. The continuing threat of a nuclear strike was designed to force the North Vietnamese to negotiate.

## Support or challenge?

Below is a sample exam-style question which asks how far you agree with a specific statement. Below this are a series of general statements which are relevant to the question. Using your own knowledge and the information on the opposite page decide whether these statements support or challenge the statement in the question and tick the appropriate box.

'Nixon's policy of Vietnamisation was a continuation of Johnson's policy in Vietnam.' How far do you agree with this statement?

| Statement | SUPPORT | CHALLENGE |
|---|---|---|
| Nixon favoured a phased withdrawal of US troops. | | |
| Nixon wanted the ARVN to play the leading role in the fight against communism in Vietnam. | | |
| Nixon wanted US troops to focus on air warfare and technical support. | | |
| Nixon wanted to decrease anti-war feeling in the USA. | | |
| Nixon wanted to continue fighting communism in Vietnam until a peace deal was agreed. | | |
| Nixon wanted to reduce US spending on the Vietnam War. | | |

## Complete the paragraph

Below are a sample exam-style question and a paragraph written in answer to this question. The paragraph contains a point and specific examples, but lacks a concluding explanatory link back to the question. Complete the paragraph adding this link in the space provided.

Why did President Nixon introduce Vietnamisation in 1969?

> One reason why President Nixon introduced Vietnamisation in 1969 was the Guam Doctrine. Nixon's new doctrine set out a new method of opposing communism. The USA would continue to offer support in terms of military equipment and economic aid to countries fighting communism, and therefore help contain communism, which had been US policy since Truman. However, Nixon argued that the USA had no responsibility to provide ground troops. In practice, this meant that the ARVN, and not US troops, would play the leading role in the fight against communism in Vietnam.

# Section 4: The Nixon presidency and the withdrawal of US forces, 1969–73

## Achieving 'peace with honour': Nixon's military strategy

Revised

Nixon hoped to achieve 'peace with honour' by negotiating from a position of strength. He hoped that a strong military strategy would force North Vietnam to accept that they could not win the war, and therefore agree to a peace treaty on US terms.

### The successes and failures of Vietnamisation

The success of Vietnamisation was essential if Nixon was to achieve 'peace with honour'. Vietnamisation would strengthen the USA's negotiating position by increasing public support for the war in the USA without decreasing military pressure on Ho Chi Minh. However, the results of Vietnamisation were mixed.

| Successes of Vietnamisation | Failures of Vietnamisation |
| --- | --- |
| • Vietnamisation allowed US troops to begin to withdraw from South Vietnam. The first withdrawals began in September 1969, earlier than the public had thought possible. By the end of 1970, 150,000 US troops had left Vietnam. By December 1971, the US force in Vietnam had been reduced to 140,000.<br>• Nixon announced the different waves of withdrawal at strategic intervals in order to undermine the anti-war movement in the USA.<br>• The ARVN grew from 850,000 to 1,000,000.<br>• Nixon continued the Phoenix Program (see page 38), handing over responsibility for the programme to the ARVN. The programme became more sophisticated, capturing greater numbers of Viet Cong leaders. | • The ARVN struggled to keep hold of recruits, with many soldiers deserting. Between 1969 and 1973, an average of 100,000 ARVN troops deserted every year.<br>• In 1971, the ARVN attacked communists in Laos as part of their attack on the Ho Chi Minh Trail. In spite of high-tech US equipment, the ARVN were forced to retreat.<br>• The speedy withdrawal of US troops diminished the morale of the troops who remained. US troops no longer felt committed to fighting the war once the policy of withdrawal had been initiated. |

### US airpower

Part of Vietnamisation was the continued use of US airpower. Nixon decided to extend the USA's bombing campaign to Cambodia and Laos in order to disrupt the Ho Chi Minh Trail (see map on page 22). The Ho Chi Minh Trail allowed the NVA to supply its troops in South Vietnam. Therefore, bombing the trail was designed to make NVA operations in South Vietnam more difficult.

#### Covert bombings

Nixon kept his bombing campaign a secret. He feared the public would not support his actions against Cambodia and Laos. Additionally, bombing Cambodia and Laos was illegal under the terms of the Geneva Accords as both countries were technically neutral. Nonetheless, as both countries had already broken the terms of the Accords by allowing the NVA to operate in their territory, Nixon knew that they would not complain to the UN.

The bombing of Cambodia began in March 1969, and intensified between April and June. The bombing of Laos began in February 1970.

#### The impact of the bombings

The bombing raids failed to stop the NVA's attacks on the South. In addition, Nixon was forced to inform the US public about the bombing in April 1969. The public were confused by the apparent contradiction between Nixon's claim that he was seeking peace in Vietnam, and the act of extending the war. As a result, anti-war feeling increased.

## Delete as applicable

Below are a sample exam-style question and a paragraph written in answer to this question. Read the paragraph and decide which of the possible options (in bold) is most appropriate. Delete the least appropriate options and complete the paragraph by justifying your selection.

How successful was the US policy of Vietnamisation in the years 1969–73?

> In terms of withdrawing US troops from Vietnam, the US policy of Vietnamisation was successful to a **great/fair/limited** extent. For example, Nixon was able to begin troop withdrawals in September 1969, earlier than the public had anticipated. By the end of 1970, 150,000 US troops had been withdrawn from Vietnam. A year later, the US force was reduced to a mere 140,000 men. Nixon achieved this by enlarging the ARVN from 850,000 to 1,000,000 men. In this way, in terms of withdrawing US troops from Vietnam, the US policy of Vietnamisation was successful to a **great/fair/limited** extent because
>
> _____
>
> _____

## Eliminate irrelevance

Below are a sample exam-style question and a paragraph written in answer to this question. Read the paragraph and identify parts of the paragraph that are not directly relevant to the question. Draw a line through the information that is irrelevant and justify your deletions in the margin.

How successful was the US policy of Vietnamisation in the years 1969–73?

> Vietnamisation was essentially a continuation of Johnson's policy of de-Americanisation, which was adopted after the Tet Offensive of 1968. Nixon was committed to Vietnamisation because of his Guam Doctrine which said that US troops should not do the majority of fighting in Vietnam. In terms of troop morale, Nixon's policy of Vietnamisation was a significant failure. Withdrawing large numbers of US troops from Vietnam, with the aim of withdrawing all troops from Vietnam as fast as possible, meant that those who stayed behind were no longer committed to fighting the war. This was because they knew that the end of the war was in sight and they wanted to return home rather than risking their lives for a war that the USA was no longer interested in fighting. This was unlike the Korean War in which morale stayed high due to the fact that US soldiers were fighting a conventional battle. Morale within the ARVN was also low and, on average, the ARVN lost 100,000 troops a year from desertion. In this way, Vietnamisation failed in its aim of maintaining pressure on the NVA to a large extent because of poor morale amongst US and ARVN troops.

**Section 4:** The Nixon presidency and the withdrawal of US forces, 1969–73

## Achieving 'peace with honour': Nixon's diplomatic strategy

There were two strands to Nixon's diplomatic strategy:

- He aimed to relax tensions between the USA and the Soviet Union and China in the hope that the Soviet Union and China would put pressure on North Vietnam to negotiate an end to the war.
- He opened secret negotiations between US officials and North Vietnamese officials.

### The changing Cold War context

Nixon had a new approach to the Cold War known as 'realpolitik'. It meant that he was willing to open a dialogue with the Soviet Union and China rather than treating them as ideological enemies. This policy led to an improvement in relations between the USA and the major communist powers. The improvement in relations with the Soviet Union was known as **détente**.

### Secret negotiations

Nixon began secret talks with leading members of the North Vietnamese government.

- In May 1969, Nixon published an eight-point programme designed to be the basis of peace talks. Ho Chi Minh refused to provide a public response.
- In July, **Henry Kissinger**, Nixon's National Security Advisor, began peace talks with Xuan Thuy, a senior member of the North Vietnamese government, at a secret meeting in Paris.
- In October 1970, Nixon proposed a ceasefire and offered a peace settlement which would allow North Vietnam to retain the territory it had conquered in the South. The North Vietnamese rejected the settlement.

Negotiations stalled because the North Vietnamese wanted the USA to agree to remove Nguyen Van Thieu as leader of South Vietnam. Kissinger refused, arguing that the USA had no authority to replace the South Vietnamese leader.

North Vietnamese leaders believed that they were in a strong position as US opposition to the war would put pressure on Nixon to accept peace at any price. Indeed, the NVA deliberately adopted a strategy of maximising the number of US soldiers killed to heighten anti-war feeling in the USA. As a result, North Vietnam felt no pressure to accept US terms.

### Ho Chi Minh's death

Ho Chi Minh died in September 1969. He was succeeded by his Vice-President, Ton Duc Thang.

### How successful was Nixon's strategy?

By 1972, détente was clearly successful. The Soviet Union and the USA agreed an **Arms Limitation Treaty** and an **Agreement on Basic Principles** which stabilised relationships within the Cold War. At the same time, Nixon met with Mao Zedong and established a working relationship between the USA and China.

Nevertheless, the Soviet Union did nothing to bring about an end to the Vietnam War. Mao Zedong was much more helpful and personally told Pham Van Dong, the North Vietnamese Prime Minister, to reach a compromise with the USA.

Thang, the new President of North Vietnam, was aware of the new Cold War context and feared that he would lose the support of the Soviet Union and China if he continued to fight. However, rather than being persuaded to negotiate, Thang tried to sabotage détente by launching the Spring Offensive of 1972 (see page 56).

## Spectrum of significance

Below are a sample exam-style question and a list of general points which could be used to answer the question. Use your own knowledge and the information in Sections 3 and 4 so far to reach a judgement about the importance of these general points to the question posed. Write numbers on the spectrum below to indicate their relative importance. Having done this, write a brief justification of your placement, explaining why some of these factors are more important than others. The resulting diagram could form the basis of an essay plan.

> How far do you agree that the Tet Offensive was the main reason for the withdrawal of US troops from Vietnam in the period 1969–73?

1. The Tet Offensive
2. Nixon's policy of détente
3. US public opinion
4. The Guam Doctrine
5. The financial cost of the war
6. Nixon had no other viable options

⟵―――――――――――――――――――⟶

Very important                                    Less important

## You're the examiner

Below are a sample exam-style question and a paragraph written in answer to this question. Read the paragraph and the mark scheme provided on page 3. Decide which level you would award the paragraph. Write the level below, along with a justification for your choice.

> How far do you agree that the Tet Offensive was the main reason for the withdrawal of US troops from Vietnam in the period 1969–73?

One reason that the USA withdrew troops from Vietnam was Nixon's policy of détente. Nixon's new policy was designed to get the USA on better terms with the Soviet Union and China, its communist enemies. Nixon's idea was known as 'realpolitik' and suggested that the USA could deal with the Soviet Union and China through negotiation rather than treating them as hostile ideological enemies with whom the USA could have no communication. Détente paid off in 1972 as the USA and the Soviet Union signed an Agreement of Basic Principles and an Arms Limitation Treaty which brought more stability to superpower relations in the Cold War.

Level:    Reason for choosing this level:
_____
_____

# Section 4: The Nixon presidency and the withdrawal of US forces, 1969–73

## The impact of the anti-war movement

### Anti-war feeling

The anti-war movement had three major sources: the Civil Rights movement, the Black Power movement, and the student movement (see page 44).

Following the Tet Offensive in 1968, there was a brief explosion of anti-war feeling which caused political problems for Johnson. Nixon was determined not to give in to anti-war protestors and, as far as possible, to conduct the war in such a way as to minimise anti-war feeling. Nonetheless, on 15 October 1969, 2 million people across 200 US cities protested against the war.

### 'The silent majority'

In spite of massive anti-war protests, as late as 1969 around 68 per cent of the US public approved of Nixon's policy in Vietnam. Nixon described this as 'the silent majority'. He also argued that anti-war protests were pointless as the government would never give in to popular pressure while it had the backing of the 'silent majority'. Nixon's tough stance on the war appeared to have won him a great deal of support. Indeed, he won the 1972 Presidential election with a landslide victory.

### Causes of anti-war feeling during Nixon's presidency

The following events had a significant impact on American perceptions of the war:

| Event | Impact on public opinion |
| --- | --- |
| The My Lai Massacre (March 1968) | In March 1968, a routine 'clear and hold' operation led to the massacre of more than 300 Vietnamese civilians. The event was covered up by Johnson's administration. However, it was made public by *LIFE* Magazine in December 1969. This caused concern amongst the US public because it was clear that US soldiers were behaving cruelly. It called into question the morality of the war. |
| The Kent State Massacre (May 1970) | When news of the bombing of Cambodia became public, students at Kent State University in Ohio protested. Four were shot and killed and nine were wounded by the National Guard. In response, demonstrations against the treatment of protestors broke out across the USA. |
| The Pentagon Papers (July 1971) | In July 1971, the *New York Times* published parts of a leaked report entitled 'US–Vietnam Relations, 1945–1967'. The report had been commissioned by Robert McNamara. The *New York Times* showed that Johnson and Kennedy had lied to the public about US involvement in Vietnam and the possibilities of success. |

### The significance of the anti-war movement

After the Tet Offensive, public opposition to the war convinced Nixon that the USA should withdraw from major combat operations in Vietnam. In this sense, public pressure played a role in shaping the overall direction of US policy.

However, Nixon knew that he had the backing of the majority of Americans and that black radicals and student radicals did not represent majority opinion in the USA. Therefore, Nixon did not rush into a humiliating peace deal in order to win their support.

Nonetheless, Nixon did time his public announcements to undermine the anti-war movement. For example, Nixon's announcement of the withdrawal of 25,000 men from Vietnam in June 1969 and his announcement that the USA had been engaged in secret peace talks were deliberately designed to show that the government was working for peace and that anti-war protestors were overreacting.

## Simple essay style

Below is a sample exam-style question. Use your own knowledge and the information on the opposite page to produce a plan for an answer to this question. Choose four general points, and provide three pieces of specific information to support each general point. Once you have planned your essay, write the introduction and conclusion for the essay. The introduction should list the points to be discussed in the essay. The conclusion should summarise the key points and justify which point was the most important.

> How far do you agree that popular protest in the USA was the main reason for the gradual withdrawal of US troops from Vietnam in the years 1969–73?

## Develop the detail (a)

Below are a sample exam-style question and a paragraph written in answer to this question. The paragraph contains a limited amount of detail. Annotate the paragraph to add additional detail to the answer.

> How far do you agree that popular protest in the USA was the main reason for the gradual withdrawal of US troops from Vietnam in the years 1968–73?

> Popular protest was certainly the main reason for the gradual withdrawal of US troops from Vietnam in the years 1968–73. Several groups opposed the war in Vietnam. There were many protests in these years, often involving a great many people. Also, there were scandals in the press. In addition, the handling of the protests led to greater anti-war feeling. Furthermore, famous personalities came out in opposition to the war. In this way, popular protest was the main reason for the withdrawal of US troops from Vietnam because the withdrawal minimised opposition to the war and maximised Nixon's chances of re-election.

## Recommended reading

Below is a list of suggested further reading on this topic.

- Steve Phillips, *The Cold War: Conflict in Europe and Asia* (pages 93–100). Heinemann, 2001.
- Martin McCauley, *Russia, America and the Cold War 1949–91* (pages 58–59). Longman, 2004.
- Hugh Brogan, *The Penguin History of the United States of America* (pages 683–689). Penguin, 1990.

Section 4: The Nixon presidency and the withdrawal of US forces, 1969–73

# The end of the Vietnam War

## Nixon's successes by 1972

By early 1972, Nixon's policy was clearly showing some success:

- The USA had fewer than 100,000 troops in Vietnam.
- The ARVN was able to conduct competent defensive operations.
- The 'clear and hold' policy had secured more than 50 per cent of the farmland in South Vietnam.
- Détente had led to high level talks between the USA and its communist rivals.

## Congressional opposition

Despite Nixon's successes, Nixon faced increasing opposition from **Congress**. America's political elite felt that Nixon was abusing his power as Commander-in-Chief. Consequently, Congress passed a series of laws restricting the president's power to wage war in Vietnam. In January 1971, Congress **repealed** the Gulf of Tonkin Resolution. Additionally, between April and July 1971, Congress passed seventeen laws restricting US involvement in the war in Vietnam. Congress also refused to continue funding the war.

## The Spring Offensive

In March 1972, Thang launched a new offensive, timed to coincide with the US Presidential Election Campaign. Thang hoped that Nixon would want to conclude peace before the election in November.

Initially, the Spring Offensive was very successful and by 1 May 1972, the NVA captured Quang Tri, a major city in South Vietnam.

### Nixon's response

Nixon's campaign for re-election was very successful and therefore he felt no pressure to agree a peace deal before November. Rather, he authorised a counter-attack which successfully repelled the Spring Offensive.

## The final peace negotiations

### October talks

In October 1972, a provisional peace deal was agreed. The USA agreed to the following terms:

- the withdrawal of all US troops
- an immediate ceasefire
- North Vietnam would keep all territory conquered in South Vietnam
- that no further military aid would be given to South Vietnam.

North Vietnam agreed:

- to return all US prisoners of war
- that the military government of Thieu would continue ruling South Vietnam.

### The breakdown of talks

Thang withdrew from negotiations when he discovered that Nixon and Kissinger had assured Thieu that they would continue to send military aid to South Vietnam.

### Operation Linebacker II (December 1972)

In order to force Thang to negotiate, Nixon authorised Operation Linebacker II, the 'Christmas bombings'. The bombing campaign targeted the cities of Hanoi and Haiphong.

### Final peace

A ceasefire was agreed, beginning on 27 January 1973, and US troops were given 60 days to withdraw. The terms agreed at the October talks formed the basis for the peace deal, but in addition Nixon agreed not to supply the South Vietnamese government with new weaponry. This allowed him to continue 'replacing' South Vietnam's existing stocks of weapons.

## Did Nixon achieve 'peace with honour'?

Nixon succeeded in withdrawing US troops from Vietnam. He also succeeded in giving the South Vietnamese government, in Kissinger's words, a 'fighting chance' of survival. Nonetheless, the USA lost 58,000 soldiers in Vietnam, and 3 million Vietnamese lives were lost. Furthermore, US servicemen often suffered from psychological damage as a result of their experiences in the Vietnam War. Finally, the war demonstrated that the richest and possibly most powerful country in the world could not score a decisive victory against poorly-trained and poorly-equipped guerrilla fighters.

## RAG – Rate the timeline

Below are a sample exam-style question and a timeline. Read the question, study the timeline and, using three coloured pens, put a red, amber or green star next to the events to show:

- red – events and policies that have no relevance to the question
- amber – events and policies that have some significance to the question
- green – events and policies that are directly relevant to the question.

1. Why did it take Nixon so long to achieve the complete withdrawal of US troops from Vietnam?

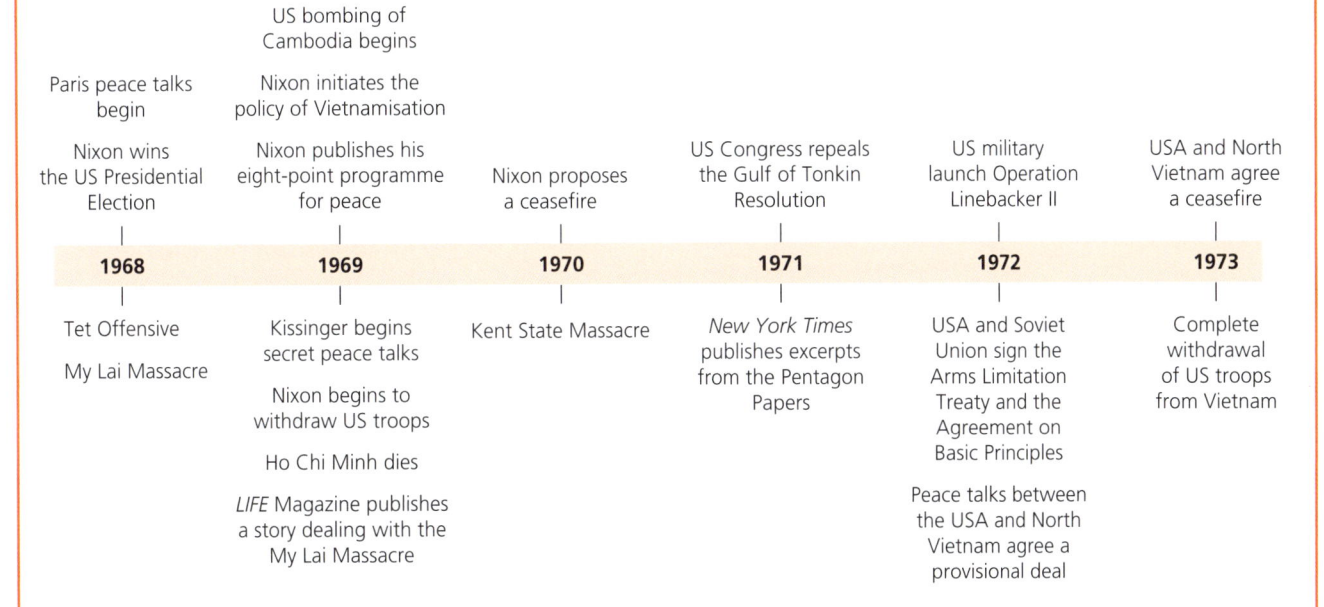

**1968**
- Paris peace talks begin
- Nixon wins the US Presidential Election
- Tet Offensive
- My Lai Massacre

**1969**
- US bombing of Cambodia begins
- Nixon initiates the policy of Vietnamisation
- Nixon publishes his eight-point programme for peace
- Kissinger begins secret peace talks
- Nixon begins to withdraw US troops
- Ho Chi Minh dies
- LIFE Magazine publishes a story dealing with the My Lai Massacre

**1970**
- Nixon proposes a ceasefire
- Kent State Massacre

**1971**
- US Congress repeals the Gulf of Tonkin Resolution
- New York Times publishes excerpts from the Pentagon Papers

**1972**
- US military launch Operation Linebacker II
- USA and Soviet Union sign the Arms Limitation Treaty and the Agreement on Basic Principles
- Peace talks between the USA and North Vietnam agree a provisional deal

**1973**
- USA and North Vietnam agree a ceasefire
- Complete withdrawal of US troops from Vietnam

Now repeat the activity with the following questions. You could use different colours, or number your stars 1, 2 or 3.

2. How far was the dominance of US airpower in the years 1969–73 the main reason that North Vietnam agreed to an armistice in 1973?
3. How far had Nixon achieved 'peace with honour' in Vietnam by 1973?

## Complex essay style

Below are a sample exam-style question, a list of key points to be made in the essay, and a simple introduction and conclusion for the essay. Read the question, the key points, and the introduction and conclusion. Rewrite the introduction and the conclusion in order to develop an argument.

> How far were growing doubts within the political elite the main reason for the gradual withdrawal of US troops from Vietnam during 1969–73?

### Key points

- Growing doubts within the political elite
- The Tet Offensive
- Popular protest
- The cost of the war
- Quagmire Theory
- The Guam Doctrine

### Introduction

*There were six key reasons for the gradual withdrawal of US troops from Vietnam in the years 1969–73. These were growing doubts within the political elite, the Tet Offensive, popular protest, the cost of the war, the Quagmire Theory, and the Guam Doctrine.*

### Conclusion

*There were six key reasons for the gradual withdrawal of US troops from Vietnam in the years 1969–73. The most important reason was the growing doubts within the political elite. This played a more significant role than all of the other factors.*

# Section 4: The Nixon presidency and the withdrawal of US forces, 1969–73

## Exam focus

Below is a sample A-grade essay. Read it and the examiner's comments around it.

How far do you agree that the Tet Offensive was the main reason for the withdrawal of US troops from Vietnam in the years 1968–1973?

The withdrawal of US troops from Vietnam in the years 1968–1973 was largely due to the policies of President Nixon rather than the Tet Offensive. The Tet Offensive created an initial shock which set the direction of US policy, but it was not until the election of President Nixon in 1968 that the US government began to develop a policy that would allow US troops to withdraw.

*The introduction focuses on the question and outlines the argument. However, it does not set out the factors that will be discussed in the essay.*

The Tet Offensive of 1968 was undoubtedly one reason for the withdrawal of US troops from Vietnam. Although the USA won the final victory, the sight of NVA troops surrounding the US Embassy in Saigon, and the obvious failure of US intelligence, which had been focusing on the Khe Sanh Offensive, humiliated the US government and persuaded the US public that the Vietnam War could not be won. From that point on President Johnson started a policy of de-Americanisation and scaled back the US effort in Vietnam. However, the Tet Offensive did not cause the immediate withdrawal of US troops. Indeed, the first US troops did not leave Vietnam until September 1969. In this way, the Tet Offensive caused a change in US policy but it was not solely responsible for the withdrawal of US troops from Vietnam.

*This paragraph is full of detailed information and the makes correct use of technical terms such as de-Americanisation. This shows detailed and accurate knowledge of the topic.*

Nixon's policies were the key reason for the withdrawal of US troops from Vietnam. Nixon was elected with a mandate to achieve 'peace with honour'. On taking office, Nixon set out the Guam Doctrine, a statement that the USA would continue to support the fight against communism, but that US troops would no longer be deployed on the front line against communist forces. Nixon began withdrawing troops in September 1969. By the end of 1970, 150,000 US troops had been withdrawn from Vietnam, and by the end of 1971, there were only 140,000 US troops left in Vietnam. In this way, Nixon's policies were the key reason for the withdrawal of US troops because, in line with the Guam Doctrine, they aimed to shift the burden of fighting communism from the USA to local forces within Vietnam.

*This paragraph advances the argument set out in the introduction by explaining why Nixon's policies were more important than the Tet Offensive.*

The withdrawal of US troops was achieved through the policy of Vietnamisation. This new policy meant that the USA played an increasingly supportive role while the ARVN began to take on the responsibility for fighting communism. As part of the policy, the

ARVN increased in size from 850,000 to 1,000,000. At the same time, the remaining US troops supported them by fighting the air war against North Vietnam. In this sense, Vietnamisation was the method that Nixon used to withdraw troops, rather than the cause of the withdrawal.

US public opinion also played a role in the decision to withdraw US troops from Vietnam. Following the Tet Offensive, opposition to the war increased amongst the US population. Prior to the Tet Offensive, opposition mainly came from radical political groups such as the Black Power movement and SDS. However, following the Tet Offensive, opposition became more widespread. Indeed, in October 1969, 2 million people across 200 US cities took part in a mass protest against the war. Opposition increased following the Kent State Massacre and stories in the press about the My Lai Massacre. However, opposition was not the primary cause of the withdrawal from Vietnam as, at the same time, around 68 per cent of people approved of Nixon's policy in the region. What is more, Nixon had other policies, such as pulling US troops out of combat roles, which reduced opposition to the war without withdrawing troops from Vietnam. In this way, US public opinion was not the main reason for the withdrawal of troops because Nixon was able to persuade the majority of the public that he was pursuing the right policy in Vietnam.

In conclusion, the Tet Offensive was not the main reason for the withdrawal of US troops from Vietnam — although it caused a big shift in US public opinion, it did not lead to the immediate withdrawal of US troops. The withdrawal only happened after the election of Nixon and a change in US policy.

> Here, the candidate weighs up the importance of public opinion. The paragraph ends by explaining why this factor is less important than Nixon's policies. In this sense, it continues the argument set out in the introduction.

> The conclusion rounds off the argument that Nixon was more important than the Tet Offensive. However, it does not make any reference to the importance of the other factors discussed in the essay.

**26/30**
This essay is awarded a mark low in Level 5. It reaches Level 5 due to the sustained argument which runs through every paragraph of the essay. However, it remains low in the Level for two reasons. First, the introduction and conclusion do not consider the full range of factors discussed in the essay. Secondly, the essay does not consider some important factors, such as Congressional opposition to the war, and consequently lacks range.

### What makes a good answer?

You have now considered four sample A-grade essays (see pages 16, 26, 46 and above). Use these essays to make a bullet-pointed list of the characteristics of an A-grade essay. Use this list when planning and writing your own practice exam essays.

# Glossary

**17th Parallel** The provisional border between North and South Vietnam, established by the Geneva Accords. It ran along the circle of latitude 17 degrees north of the equator.

**38th Parallel** The provisional border between North and South Korea agreed in 1945. It ran along the circle of latitude 38 degrees north of the equator.

**Agent Orange** A toxic chemical used to kill trees during the Vietnam War. The aim was to destroy the jungle cover of the Viet Cong.

**Agreement on Basic Principles** An agreement signed by the USA and the Soviet Union in 1972, which agreed the fundamental principles which should govern superpower relations.

**armistice** An agreement to stop fighting.

**Arms Limitation Treaty** An agreement signed by the USA and the Soviet Union in 1972, which agreed small-scale reductions in the number of nuclear weapons held by the two superpowers.

**arms race** A situation where a number of powers expand their military forces as they compete for dominance.

**Army of the Republic of Vietnam (ARVN)** The South Vietnamese army.

**Axis Powers** An alliance comprising Germany, Italy and Japan that fought the allies during the Second World War.

**Black Power movement** A movement emerging in 1966, dedicated to the fight for black rights. In contrast to the Civil Rights movement, members of the Black Power movement were willing to use violence to achieve racial equality.

**budget deficit** Government debt.

**buffer zone** A geographical area that lies between two hostile states.

**China Lobby** A group of US politicians who responded to the fall of China to communism by criticising Truman's handling of the Cold War and demanding a tougher stance against communism.

**CIA** The Counter-Intelligence Agency: the US government organisation tasked with protecting the USA from foreign threats.

**colonial rule** The rule of an empire.

**colonialism** *See* imperialism.

**Commitment Trap** The theory that as soon as the USA became involved in fighting communism in Vietnam, they were unable to withdraw due to the fact that they could neither win nor lose face. *See also* Quagmire Theory.

**Congress** The American Parliament.

**Congressional elections** Elections to the American Parliament.

**Congressman** Member of the American Parliament.

**conventional forces** Members of a professionally trained army.

**covert operations** Secret military missions.

**defoliants** Chemicals that destroy plants.

**Demilitarised Zone (DMZ)** An area in which no weapons or armed forces are permitted.

**Democratic Party** The Democratic Party is one of the two main political parties in modern America.

**Democratic People's Republic of Korea (DPRK)** North Korea.

**détente** A period of decreased tension between the USA and the Soviet Union during the Cold War. It is traditionally dated from 1970 to 1976.

**Domino Theory** The belief that the fall of any one state to communism in south-east Asia would inevitably lead to the spread of communism across the region.

**Douglas MacArthur** A senior US military officer who played a prominent role during the Second World War in the Pacific. He later commanded UNC troops during the Korean War.

**draft card** An official card sent by the US government to young men informing them that they were eligible to be called up to fight in the Vietnam War.

**fragging** Attacking a senior officer with the intent of killing him.

**Gross National Product (GNP)** The total wealth produced by a country in a specific period.

**Grand Alliance** The alliance between the USA, the Soviet Union and the United Kingdom during the Second World War.

**Great Society Programme** President Johnson's programme of social reform designed to redistribute wealth and increase equality of opportunity in the USA.

**guerrilla** Unconventional warfare commonly used by inferior forces against better equipped armies. Guerrilla fighters hide and launch surprise attacks.

**Henry Kissinger** President Nixon's National Security Advisor, and later Secretary of State. Together with Nixon, he is credited with developing the policy of détente.

**Ho Chi Minh Trail** The supply lines running through Cambodia and Laos that allowed the Viet Cong and the NVA to operate so successfully in South Vietnam.

**imperialism** Also known as colonialism. The policy and idea of pursuing the creation and maintenance of an empire. Imperialism also relates to the ideas that might be used to justify such a policy.

**installations** Military bases.

**land reform** The policy of redistributing land from wealthy landowners to the peasants.

**Malayan Emergency** An anti-colonial struggle fought between the Malayan National Liberation Army and the forces of the British Empire. The Emergency lasted from 1948 until 1960.

**Martin Luther King** The most prominent US black civil rights campaigner. He led a number of important campaigns between 1955 and 1968.

**militia** Non-professional soldiers.

**Napalm** A highly flammable and sticky chemical jelly. The USA used it to destroy areas of jungle during the Vietnam War.

**nationalist** A person who believes that their nation should be self-governing.

**NATO** The North Atlantic Treaty Organisation. Founded in 1949, it was designed to provide security for Western Europe during the Cold War.

**nuclear parity** A situation in which two nuclear powers have roughly equal numbers of nuclear weapons.

**Pacific Defensive Perimeter** A geographical area in the Western Pacific in which the USA was committed to providing security against communism.

**Pacific Rim** The countries bordering the Pacific Ocean.

**pitched battle** A planned battle.

**proxy war** A war in which superpowers fight each other indirectly, using small powers as substitutes.

**Quagmire Theory** The theory that the USA had become entrapped in Vietnam, and was unable to withdraw.

**reconnaissance** Spying.

**referendum** A popular vote on a specific issue.

**repatriate** Return a person to their country of origin.

**repeal** To remove of a law.

**Republic of Korea (ROK)** South Korea.

**Republican Party** One of the two main political parties in modern America.

**rollback** The policy of liberating territory from communist influence.

**satellite state** A state that is formally independent, but heavily influenced by another state.

**self-immolation** Setting oneself on fire.

**signatories** People who sign a document or agreement.

**Soviet Union** A group of communist countries dominated by Russia. One of the two superpowers during the Cold War.

**Special Forces** Elite military troops.

**sphere of influence** A geographical area in which one country dominates.

**Stalin** The leader of the Soviet Union from 1928 until 1953.

**strategic hamlets** Villages fortified to protect them against the Viet Cong.

**Students for a Democratic Society (SDS)** An organisation of radical students formed in the USA in 1960.

**superpower** A term used to describe the USA and the Soviet Union after the Second World War due to their military, economic and political dominance.

**Taiwan** An island off the south-east coast of communist China.

**teach-in** A form of protest in which students and teachers take over a university. Teach-ins are different to regular lectures as they usually focus on radical subjects.

**United Nations (UN)** An international organisation set up in 1945. The UN promotes co-operation between the countries of the world with the aim of ensuring world peace.

**Viet Cong** South Vietnamese citizens fighting on the side of the communists during the Vietnam War. The Viet Cong were known for their guerrilla tactics.

**Viet Minh** A communist and nationalist army that fought for the independence of Vietnam prior to the Geneva Accords.

**Walter Cronkite** An influential US news anchor.

**war of attrition** A prolonged conflict in which each side is gradually worn down.

**William Westmoreland** Leader of the US Army in Vietnam from 1964 until 1968.

**wise men** A group of advisors to President Johnson.

# Timeline

**1945** Harry S. Truman becomes US President

The Grand Alliance defeats the Axis Powers at the end of the Second World War

The Viet Minh declare the independence of Vietnam from French control

Korea divided at the 38th Parallel

**1947** The Red Scare begins in the USA

**1948** Beginning of the Malayan Emergency

Stalin supports the creation of a communist state in North Korea

**1949** The Soviet Union successfully tests its first nuclear bomb

Mao Zedong establishes the People's Republic of China

The China Lobby accuses Truman of 'losing China'

**1950** Dean Acheson states that Korea is outside the USA's Pacific Defensive Perimeter

Mao and Stalin sign the Treaty of Friendship, Alliance and Mutual Assistance between the Soviet Union and China

NSC-68 sets out US strategy in the Cold War

Kim Il-Sung meets Stalin in Moscow

Truman authorises US financial involvement in Vietnam

Kim Il-Sung orders the invasion of South Korea

The UN authorises the deployment of troops in Korea

Chinese volunteers enter the Korean War

**1951** Truman sacks General MacArthur

Negotiations begin between North and South Korea

**1953** Dwight D. Eisenhower becomes US President

Death of Stalin

End of the Korean War: armistice deal signed

**1954** Battle of Dien Bien Phu

The Geneva Conference agrees the Geneva Accords

Vietnam is temporarily divided

Diem becomes Prime Minister of southern Vietnam

Creation of SEATO

**1955** Referendum on the creation of South Vietnam

Diem becomes President of South Vietnam

**1956** Proposed elections across Vietnam fail to happen

**1961** John F. Kennedy becomes US President

Kennedy sends advisors to Laos

NSAM 52 sets out US policy in Vietnam

Kennedy sends US Special Forces to train the ARVN

**1962** Kennedy launches Operation Ranch Hand

US advisors recommend the creation of 'strategic hamlets'

**1963** Battle of Ap Bac

Self-immolation of Thich Quang Duc

Diem overthrown in a coup

Kennedy is assassinated

Lyndon B. Johnson becomes US President

**1964** Johnson initiates 'covert operations' in Vietnam

Gulf of Tonkin Incident

Gulf of Tonkin Resolution

**1965** Johnson launches Operation Rolling Thunder

First US ground troops arrive in Vietnam

General Westmoreland commits US troops to 'search and destroy' missions

SDS organise a 20,000-strong anti-war rally in Washington DC

Battle of Chu Lai

**1966** Escalation of US bombing in Vietnam

**1967** Martin Luther King speaks out against the Vietnam War

Johnson launches the Phoenix Program

South Vietnamese election reveals little support for the US-backed government

Battle of Khe Sanh

**1968** Tet Offensive

Mini-Tet

My Lai Massacre

|  | |  | |
|---|---|---|---|
| | Paris peace talks begin | **1971** | US Congress repeals the Gulf of Tonkin Resolution |
| | Tet III | | |
| | Nixon wins the US Presidential Election | | *New York Times* publishes excerpts from the Pentagon Papers |
| **1969** | US bombing of Cambodia begins | **1972** | USA and Soviet Union sign the Arms Limitation Treaty and the Agreement on Basic Principles |
| | Nixon initiates the policy of Vietnamisation | | |
| | Nixon publishes his eight-point programme for peace | | |
| | | | North Vietnam launches the Spring Offensive |
| | Kissinger begins secret peace talks | | Peace talks between the USA and North Vietnam agree a provisional deal |
| | Nixon begins to withdraw US troops | | |
| | Ho Chi Minh dies | | Nixon re-elected as US President |
| | Ton Duc Thang becomes President of North Vietnam | | US military launch Operation Linebacker II |
| | | **1973** | USA and North Vietnam agree a ceasefire |
| | *LIFE* Magazine publishes a story dealing with the My Lai Massacre | | Complete withdrawal of US troops from Vietnam |
| **1970** | US bombing of Laos begins | **1975** | North Vietnam launches an invasion of South Vietnam |
| | Nixon proposes a ceasefire | | |
| | Kent State Massacre | **1976** | Vietnam reunited under a communist government |

# Answers

## Section 1: The Korean War, 1950–53: causes, course and consequences

### Page 5, Complete the paragraph: suggested answer

One reason why the USA intervened in the Korean War was superpower competition during the Cold War. For example, after the Second World War a rivalry developed between the USA and the Soviet Union. This rivalry was partly ideological and based on a clash between capitalist and communist systems. The US capitalist system was characterised by political democracy, individual rights, and a large amount of economic freedom. In contrast, the Soviet Union's communist system was dominated by a single political party, which restricted the political and economic freedom of its citizens. Both superpowers gained spheres of influence following the Second World War and the two rivals competed to protect and extend their geographical influence. **In this way, one of the reasons that the USA intervened in Korea was superpower competition because the USA wanted to stop the Soviet Union from expanding its influence in East Asia.**

### Page 5, Spot the mistake

The paragraph does not get into Level 4 because it is not clearly focused on the question. Rather, it gives the background to the Korean War.

### Page 9, Eliminate irrelevance

One reason why Truman became involved in the Korean War in 1950 was to contain communism in East Asia. Truman knew that the North Korean invasion had communist Russia's backing. Truman was committed to standing up to communism, a policy known as 'containment'. ~~Also, the Republic of Korea, also known as South Korea, was struggling due to Syngman Rhee's government, which was corrupt and repressive~~. Additionally, Truman had been criticised by the China Lobby for 'losing China' to communism in 1949. Therefore, he was under pressure to act strongly in East Asia to resist the spread of communism. ~~Communists believed that single-party government was better than political democracy and that the government should control the economy~~. In this way, Truman became involved in the Korean War because he was committed to preventing the spread of communism.

### Page 11, Develop the detail: suggested answer

One reason why the Korean War developed into a stalemate in 1951 was the entry of China into the war. Chinese **volunteer** troops entered the Korean War to support the communists **in North Korea**. They were helped by the Soviet Union **which provided limited air support behind enemy lines**. The number of Chinese troops, **initially 200,000,** helped to balance the strength of the opposing **UNC** forces **under MacArthur**, and the Chinese soldiers advanced quickly**, entering the war on 26 November 1950**. In this way, China's entry into the Korean War contributed to the stalemate as it increased the forces opposing the UNC troops.

### Page 13, Identify an argument

Paragraph 1 contains the argument.

### Page 15, Turning assertion into argument: suggested answer

The USA was successful in the Korean War in the sense that **it contained communism in line with Truman's initial war objectives.**

The USA was unsuccessful in the Korean War in the sense that **it failed to roll back communism in East Asia, and the war was costly in economic and human terms.**

China was partially successful in the Korean War in the sense that **while the Chinese army showed that it was a match for US forces, the war was of huge human and economic cost to China.**

### Page 15, You're the examiner

The paragraph should be awarded Level 3 because it has a general point that is focused on the question, and attempts analysis in the final sentence. However, the supporting information tells the story of the Korean War rather than providing an answer to the question.

## Section 2: The ideological struggle in south-east Asia in the early 1950s

### Page 19, Eliminate irrelevance

One reason for US intervention in south-east Asia between 1950 and 1954 was the decline of imperialism in the region. ~~For example, the Japanese Empire had lost control of Korea at the end of the Second World War~~. Following the Second World War, Ho Chi Minh and the Viet Minh were extremely successful in waging a guerrilla war against the French Empire. Similarly, the British Empire was under threat from Chin Peng's Malayan National Liberation Army in Malaya. ~~Britain and the USA had both been part of the Grand Alliance, along with the Soviet Union, during the Second World War~~. Both the Viet Minh and the MNLA were communist, and their struggle for national liberation led to an increase in their support. In this way, the decline of imperialism led to US intervention in south-east Asia because the USA feared that the struggle against imperialism was leading to the growth of communism in south-east Asia.

## Page 21, Complete the paragraph: suggested answer

One reason why the USA became increasingly involved in south-east Asia in the period 1950–1954 was the influence of the China Lobby. For example, **Truman's political enemies blamed him for not doing more to stop the communist revolution in China in 1949. The most significant member of the China Lobby was Senator Joseph McCarthy, who played a key role in the Red Scare in the USA between 1947 and 1953. McCarthy argued that Truman was doing too little and that his government was full of communist spies. McCarthy's picture of Truman's government gained strength when the Rosenbergs were convicted of giving US nuclear secrets to the Soviet Union. The China Lobby was a threat to Truman because its criticisms made his government unpopular, and Truman believed that backing military action against communism in south-east Asia would counter the criticisms.** In this way, the influence of the China Lobby led to increasing US involvement because it forced Truman to take a firm stand against communism in Asia.

## Page 23, Turning assertion into argument: suggested answer

Fear of communist expansion in Asia was one reason why Truman and Eisenhower sent aid to the French because **the USA was committed to containing communism and both presidents feared that the French would be unable to contain communism without US support**.

Political pressure in the USA was one reason why Truman sent aid to the French because **he needed to counter criticisms from the China Lobby that he was 'soft on communism' in Asia**.

Viet Minh successes were one reason why Eisenhower sent aid to the French because **he believed that the French could only defeat the Viet Minh with US support.**

## Page 25, Develop the detail: suggested answer

One reason for the establishment of SEATO in 1954 was the 'failure' of the Geneva Accords. The US President **Eisenhower** believed that the Geneva Accords **signed in May 1954** had been a failure because they failed to contain communism. Under the Accords, it had been agreed to divide Vietnam **at the 17th Parallel**, and to reunite it later **following democratic elections in 1956**. Eisenhower believed that this would lead to a communist victory in Vietnam **because Ho Chi Minh, leader of North Vietnam, was popular and the regime in South Vietnam was corrupt**. The Geneva Accords also agreed that France would leave Vietnam **in 1956** and France had been leading the fight against communism in the area. In this way, the perceived failure of the Geneva Accords led Eisenhower to seek an alternative way of containing communism in south-east Asia. Consequently, he formed SEATO.

## Section 3: Growing US participation in Vietnam, 1954–68

### Page 31, Complete the paragraph: suggested answer

One reason why the US provided support to South Vietnam in the period 1954–61 was support for Diem from the US Congress. **For example, prominent Congressmen such as Mike Mansfield and John F. Kennedy were key supporters of Ngo Dinh Diem, who had become prime minister of the southern region of Vietnam in 1954, and president in 1955. Indeed, Diem had more support from the US Congress than any other politician from South Vietnam.** Congress put pressure on Eisenhower to back Diem's regime and therefore was one reason why the USA provided support to South Vietnam in the period 1954 to 1961.

### Page 31, You're the examiner

The paragraph should be awarded a mark in Level 4 as it shows clear focus on the question and provides accurate, relevant and detailed supporting evidence.

### Page 33, Spot the mistake

The paragraph does not get into Level 4 because, although it focuses on Kennedy's reasons for involvement in south-east Asia, it does not explicitly focus on why he became increasingly involved.

## Page 33, Eliminate irrelevance

One reason why Kennedy continued US involvement in south-east Asia was his desire to counter accusations that the Democratic Party was 'soft on communism'. In 1949, Truman was accused of 'losing China' to communism due to his 'failure' to stop Mao Zedong's revolution. ~~Mao was a communist who later launched the Great Leap Forward.~~ Following the Chinese Revolution, the Republican Party accused the Democratic Party of being 'soft on communism'. In addition, Kennedy's most high-profile attempt to stand up to communism had been a failure. In April 1961, Kennedy authorised a CIA-backed invasion of communist Cuba. ~~CIA stands for the Counter-Intelligence Agency and is the US government organisation that has the job of protecting the USA from foreign threats.~~ The 1961 'Bay of Pigs Incident' was a disaster, and allowed the Republicans to criticise Kennedy's Cold War strategy. ~~France was also seen as being unable to stand up to communism because they were never able to defeat Ho Chi Minh.~~ In this way, Kennedy continued US involvement in south-east Asia in order to avoid further accusations that, as a Democrat, he was 'soft on communism'.

## Page 37, Turning assertion into argument: suggested answer

The Gulf of Tonkin incident was the main reason for the escalation of US involvement in south-east Asia in the years 1954–1965 in the sense that **it provided the US government with the political backing and legal authority to send troops to Vietnam.**

The Geneva Accords were another reason for the escalation of US involvement in south-east Asia in the years 1954–1965 in the sense that **they failed to guarantee the containment of communism and therefore Eisenhower felt that US involvement was necessary to stop the spread of communism.**

Johnson's desire not to 'lose Vietnam' was another reason for the escalation of US involvement in south-east Asia in the years 1954–1965 in the sense that **he felt under political pressure to stand up to communism and felt that this would best be achieved by sending in US troops.**

## Page 41, Identify an argument

Paragraph 1 contains the argument.

## Page 41, You're the examiner

The paragraph should be awarded Level 2 because it tells the story without addressing the question.

## Page 43, Develop the detail: suggested answer

One way in which the Tet Offensive was a turning point in the Vietnam War was that it exposed the weaknesses in the US strategy in Vietnam. The Tet Offensive **of 1968** showed the US public that enemy forces could reach important sites in South Vietnam **such as the US Embassy in Saigon**. It also showed that US intelligence had misunderstood the situation in Vietnam **when they focused on the NVA attack from Khe Sanh across the DMZ rather than anticipating an attack launched from the Ho Chi Minh Trail**. Finally, it showed that there was more to winning the Vietnam War than US generals had anticipated. **Westmoreland defended the US response to the Tet Offensive with reference to the 10:1 kill ratio, but this ignored the fact that the Offensive was a media victory for the Viet Cong.** In this way, the Tet Offensive was a turning point in the Vietnam War because it brought the weakness of US military strategy to the attention of the US public, turning many members of the public against the war.

## Section 4: The Nixon presidency and the withdrawal of US forces, 1969–73

## Page 49, Complete the paragraph: suggested answer

One reason why President Nixon introduced Vietnamisation in 1969 was the Guam Doctrine. Nixon's new doctrine set out a new method of opposing communism. The USA would continue to offer support in terms of military equipment and economic aid to countries fighting communism, and therefore help contain communism, which had been US policy since Truman. However, Nixon argued that the USA had no responsibility to provide ground troops. In practice, this meant that the ARVN, and not US troops, would play the leading role in the fight against communism in Vietnam. **In this way, the Guam Doctrine led to Vietnamisation because it provided the ideological justification for Nixon's new policy.**

## Page 51, Eliminate irrelevance

~~Vietnamisation was essentially a continuation of Johnson's policy of de-Americanisation, which was adopted after the Tet Offensive of 1968. Nixon was committed to Vietnamisation because of his Guam Doctrine which said that US troops should not do the majority of fighting in Vietnam.~~ In terms of troop morale, Nixon's policy of Vietnamisation was a significant failure. Withdrawing large numbers of US troops from Vietnam, with the aim of withdrawing all troops from Vietnam as fast as possible, meant that those who stayed behind were no longer committed to fighting the war. This was because they knew that the end of the war was in sight and they wanted to return home rather than risking their lives for a war that the USA was no longer interested in fighting. ~~This was unlike the Korean War in which morale stayed high due to the fact that US soldiers were fighting a conventional battle~~. Morale within the ARVN was also low and, on average, the ARVN lost 100,000 troops a year from desertion. In this way, Vietnamisation failed in its aim of maintaining pressure on the NVA to a large extent because of poor morale amongst US and ARVN troops.

## Page 53, You're the examiner

The paragraph should be awarded Level 3 because although it begins with a link to the question, and provides relevant examples, it does not provide analysis showing how those examples relate to the question.

## Page 55, Develop the detail: suggested answer

Popular protest was certainly the main reason for the gradual withdrawal of US troops from Vietnam in the years 1968–1973. Several groups opposed the war in Vietnam **including the Civil Rights movement, the Black Power movement, and SDS**. There were many protests in these years, often involving a great many people. **For example, on 15 October 1969, 2 million people in 200 US cities took part in anti-war protests.** Also, there were scandals in the press **such as *LIFE* Magazine's article on the My Lai Massacre and the *New York Times*' article on the Pentagon Papers**. In addition, the handling of the protests at **Kent State University in May 1970** led to greater anti-war feeling **after four protestors were killed by the National Guard**. Furthermore, famous personalities **such as Walter Cronkite and Martin Luther King** came out in opposition to the war. In this way, popular protest was the main reason for the withdrawal of US troops from Vietnam because the withdrawal minimised opposition to the war and maximised Nixon's chances of re-election.

# Notes

# Notes